IMPECCABLE

BIRDFEEDING

IMPECCABLE

How to Discourage Scuffling, Hull-Dropping, Seed-Throwing,
Unmentionable Nuisances, and Vulgar Chatter
at Your Birdfeeder

BILL ADLER, JR.

BIRDFEEDING

CHICAGO
REVIEW
PRESS

Library of Congress Cataloging-in-Publication Data

Adler, Bill, 1956-
   Impeccable birdfeeding : How to discourage scuffling, hull-dropping, seed-throwing, unmentionable nuisances, and vulgar chatter at your birdfeeder / Bill Adler, Jr.
       p.   cm.
   ISBN 1-55652-157-X : $9.95
   1. Birds—feeding and feeds. 2. Birds—Food. 3. Bird feeders. I.
Title

QL698.4.A35 1992
598'.07234—dc20   92-11293
                                                       CIP

Printed in the United States of America

5 4 3

Published in 1992 by Chicago Review Press, Incorporated
814 North Franklin Street
Chicago, IL 60610

To my favorite bird, P. Robin

ACKNOWLEDGMENTS

THANKS TO Beth Pratt-Dewey. And, as always, thanks to the crew at Chicago Review Press including Linda Matthews, Amy Teschner, Mark Suchomel, and Ellen Dessloch.

CONTENTS

1

*The Philosophy of
Neat Birdfeeding*

INTRODUCTION

STACK UP HOBBIES side by side and you'll see that there's no competition: feeding wild birds is the most enjoyable hobby there is. Just ask any bird feeder. Who can resist the multitude of colors, sounds, and shapes that float on the wind? Or watching their wonderful acrobatics? Or observing their many behaviors: each individual brings its own personality and beauty to your yard.

Birdfeeding is a nearly perfect hobby.

Perfect, but for two problems. The first, as everybody who feeds birds knows, is squirrels. Pesky and persistent, squirrels go hand in hand with birdfeeders. If you want to attract squirrels you could put out squirrel food in a squirrel feeder. But why bother? Erecting a birdfeeder is bound to attract squirrels even faster! Probably the only absolutely squirrel-proof birdfeeder is the mythical one erected on the top story of the World Trade Center. Mention squirrels to any bird feeder and you're enlisted in a half-hour discourse on the antics of these critters.

The second problem with birdfeeding is bird mess. "Bird mess," a euphemism for bird excrement, should be enlarged to include shell spillage as well. After a flock of finches has departed your feeder, you're left with sunflower shells all over the place and bird scat on everything in a ten-foot radius. Droppings on your feeder, on your lawn furniture, on your tomato plants, on your windowsill and windows, on your children if they happen to be playing nearby, on your car, on your barbecue grill. In the winter many birds thoughtfully leave behind whitish droppings that almost blend with the snow, but in the summer they aren't so kind: the berries consumed by wild birds when they aren't snacking at your feeder turn their scat purple, making your yard look like it was the scene of a fountain pen fight. The acidic content of bird droppings turns them into bird graffiti. Their outlines become etched permanently into various objects, including but not limited to your feeder. Trying to hose the stuff off later is a nearly impossible task.

Bird droppings are also dangerously unsanitary. They contain a variety of virulent bacteria such as salmonella, which can get on your hands when you're refilling your feeder and in your pets' mouths while they're sniffing around the vicinity. Droppings left on the ground create a perfect medium for a perilous brew of molds. When birds poop on the seed in the feeder, as they do when they eat, they contaminate the seeds themselves, which other birds eat, spreading disease among feathered friends. Sunflower shells scatter and lodge themselves in the ground, killing the grass and other foliage beneath them, like the Romans' scorched earth plan. Nothing worthwhile can grow where sunflower seed shells have fallen. Restricted to the immediate vicinity of your feeder, this might be a bearable by-product of feeding wild birds, but when the wind blows, these shells scatter, killing grass over a larger area. If you feed birds a blend of seeds—sunflower, millet, thistle—many birds will sift through the mix to find the particular seeds they want, discarding the rest. Seed shells and discarded seeds also provide a medium for molds and bacteria, so after a time you have a pretty noxious concoction growing beneath your feeder.

Bird mess—droppings, scattered seed, loose feathers, but especially scattered seed—are also invitations to other critters who may or may not be wanted. A squirrel or two is okay, I guess, but skunks and rats?

Wild birds may be pretty, but they aren't neat. They don't care, but you probably do. Except for squirrels, the most common complaint about feeding the birds is the disgusting mess they leave behind.

But there's no reason why birdfeeding has to be messy. There are techniques and strategies you can use to make birdfeeding as tidy a hobby as owning a cat. While you can't train birds to be meticulous, you can trick them to be that way. That's what *Impeccable Birdfeeding* is about.

For instance, if you have the room, you can bribe pesky birds into staying away from hanging feeders by providing a ground feeder with cracked corn far away from the other feeders. Or you can experiment with letting the feeder empty so that the offending flock moves onto more promising feeding grounds. Or you can become species-specific. This book describes strategies for attracting just those species of birds you want. Is it tufted titmice or cardinals you adore? *Impeccable Birdfeeding* tells you how to attract just those birds.

This is the essential birdfeeding guide for people whose yards have been devastated by bird droppings and seed scatterings. It's vital for apartment dwellers who must avoid littering the downstairs neighbor's air conditioner with bird debris. And for those people who live in apartments that don't allow window birdfeeding at all, this book is a must: birdfeeding without a mess means successful surreptitious birdfeeding.

In *Impeccable Birdfeeding* I'll talk about alleviating both bird droppings and scattered seeds. I'll be discussing both yard and window feeders. After you're finished with this book, your yard will look like a chemical lawn care company has been taking care of things.

I admit there's something incongruous about the notion of feeding birds—or any other animal—neatly. After all, the outdoors is messy, and will forever be messy. But your backyard isn't the outdoors. Not really. Not like the middle of a national forest or anyplace like that. Your backyard is a place where the out-of-doors meets the indoors. Where you invite nature to visit, to dine (on a meal you provide), and then to continue on its way. But nature doesn't necessarily know what the limits are. Leave your door open at night in the summer and your living room will be filled with moths and other insects. Leave your door open during the day and a deer might wander in. Think the dog food you've left outside is just for the dogs? Think again: there's probably a friendly family of skunks dining on the Alpo right now. Even trying to shut nature our completely has problems. Close the glass porch door—the one you've been meaning to put an owl decal on—and a bird might fly right into it: splat. (Sorry, but it does happen.)

When we feed birds we are attempting to control nature. Which is nothing new, since almost all human activities are, in some fashion, an attempt to control nature. We try to set limits when we feed birds. For example, many people try to exclude squirrels, pigeons, and other "undesirables" from their feeders. Many people try to protect the birds at their feeders and birdhouses from cats. Many people try to encourage goldfinches, while discouraging house finches. (Good luck.) And so on. Encouraging neatness at the birdfeeder is just another element of this desire to control nature. Trying to have birdfeeding without the mess is a perfectly acceptable, even desirable goal. After all, we wouldn't put a birdfeeder in the middle of our living room and keep the door open. So why not try to keep our yards and windows as neat as possible, too?

WHY BIRDFEEDING IS BETTER THAN OTHER HOBBIES

Hobby	Problem with the Hobby
Golf	You spend a lot of time looking for the little ball
Flying	Your spouse will never allow it
Stamp collecting	Too dull
Bird watching	Involves getting up early in the morning
Wine tasting	Too expensive
Race car driving	*See* Flying
Collecting beer bottles	You'll quickly run out of space
Needlepoint	Went out of fashion fifteen years ago
Hunting	*See* Bird watching

BIRDFEEDING BASICS

ONE OF THE BEAUTIES of feeding the birds is that it is a rather simple hobby to pursue. At a minimum, just throw some seed out on your porch and the birds do the rest. It can be that easy. In fact birds are going to appear no matter what you do, except, perhaps, unless you move to the middle of Manhattan. Of course, a little more sophistication helps enhance the hobby, so let me talk about the triad of birdfeeding: water, food, and shelter.

Even more than food, birds need water. Most books about birdfeeding talk about food, but if you look at the world from an avian perspective you'll quickly see that while food is fairly plentiful, water isn't that easy to come by. Birds need water for drinking and bathing. (You see, birds do have an instinct for cleanliness.) Apartment dwellers can also install birdbaths—I'll talk about this more later on.

A comprehensive birdfeeding yard or apartment will have at least one birdbath, heated if possible. While you can attract multiple species without ever providing a drop of water, a birdbath will make your yard much more interesting to the birds—and to you.

Generally, the heavier the birdbath the more durable. A well-protected bath is essential, because when birds are bathing they are most vulnerable to predators. Locate the birdbath near some trees or bushes so the birds have an escape route. Nixalite® or other spiny plastic or metal at the base of a feeder will keep cats away. Birdbaths should be at least three feet off the ground. Moving water attracts birds even faster than a still pool.

Fortunately, there are plenty of commercial birdbaths available, some heated, some not; you could make an entire hobby out of birdbaths. Baths require some maintenance and are affected by seasons, so you can't rely on the rain to maintain your bath. Heated baths are a good idea in the winter, as birds are not interested in ice-skating.

Whatever kind of bath you get, clean it often. Stagnant water breeds all sorts of bacteria, many of which are not good for birds. And if concern about birds' health isn't enough, consider this: stagnant water is also a breeding ground for mosquitoes. The bacteria that inhabit your birdbath can infect you, too. Don't ever chlorinate or add chemicals to the birdbath's water, because there a chance that you might harm the birds and other wildlife that take sips.

What about food? Birds eat a variety of fare in the wild as well as at your feeder, where, if you are like most people, you are offering some combination of black sunflower seeds, sunflower meats, thistle, shelled peanuts, whole peanuts, corn, safflower seeds, suet (beef fat), and millet. Insects and berries top off birds' appetites. Because not all birds like everything, each of these foods attracts different species. So you can regulate which kinds of wild birds frequent your feeder by selecting the appropriate food.

Most people put seed in feeders. In terms of attracting birds, it doesn't really matter much what feeder you select as long as the bird can reach the seed. (Some feeders yield a neater yard than others; more about that later.) There is, in fact, a great variety among feeders. They come in unlimited shapes and sizes and vary in their looks; durability; how many birds can eat from the feeder at the same time; what kind of seed the feeder can hold; whether the feeder is pole-mounted, window-mounted, or hangs; material the feeder is constructed from (plastic, metal, or wood); anti-squirrel defenses; ability to resist wind, rain, and snow; capacity; ease of refilling; and species that can eat from the feeder. Most feeders are multipurpose; that is, they attract a variety of birds, hold most seeds, and are relatively rugged. Some employ complex springs or weights to regulate their feeding ports. There are dozens, maybe hundreds of manufacturers of birdfeeders in the United States. Practicality and features are two criteria you can use when you select a birdfeeder; what the feeder looks like—esthetics—is another. While it's important to have a feeder that keeps water out, keeps squirrels at bay, and holds a lot of seed, it's almost more important, I think, to have a feeder that looks good in your yard. After all, if you're attracting birds because of what they look like, it doesn't make a lot of sense to have an ugly, cookie-cutter-type plastic feeder. Experimentation is often the best guide for determining the appropriate feeder for where you live.

Birdhouses are the third element of the essential triad. Birds need someplace to build nests, and they often use them for roosting in the cold winter. They'll use a tree, unless you offer them a more enticing residence. Unlike feeders, birdhouses often must be built with specific species in mind. A downy woodpecker, for example, won't nest in a house designed for a bluebird. Birds appreciate free lodging and return the favor by spending much of their time in the vicinity of your window. Purple martin houses are probably the best known. These birds love to eat mosquitoes and are very popular critters to have around. Wren houses are also easy to construct— empty milk cartons can be transformed into them. Wrens also eat insects.

Shop for a birdhouse that fits the kind of bird you want to attract. Later on I describe what you should look for when shopping for houses to attract particular species.

All feeders, baths, and houses must be cleaned regularly. Please! (If you have hungry squirrels you may be replacing your feeders regularly anyway.) Hot, soapy water is the best bet. Water with bleach added will help disinfect your equipment once a season. Before washing, feeders, baths, and houses should not be touched by human hands, not because the birds might be frightened away by your scent, but because birds carry germs. Birdfeeders are filled with dangerous germs. Bird droppings contain bacteria; birds also carry organisms on their feathers. A short list of the bacterial and fungal infections you can get from birds includes salmonellosis, encephalitis, erysipelas, histoplasmosis, botulism, and chlamydia. Wear rubber gloves when you wash your equipment. Wash your hands every time you add seed to a feeder or otherwise come in contact with the equipment. And without doubt, watch your children. They may play with the birdbath and then put their hands in their mouths. That will almost guarantee a visit to the pediatrician's office. Germs are the most powerful reason to curtail bird droppings and fallen feathers.

Reduce, or better yet, eliminate pesticides and herbicides in your yard. Even small applications will kill wild birds. Some experts blame the decrease in songbird populations on all the chemicals used on yards, farms, and gardens. Besides, most birds eat some insects, so a bug-free yard doesn't do much in the way of attracting wild birds. Pesticides and herbicides are unnecessary in most instances; nature is well equipped to take care of itself. Weeds can be killed by hand or with an electrical weed whacker. An unfortunate complication of using pesticides is that the more you use, the more you will need to use, as insects gain resistance. Birds, on the other hand, are nature's pesticide.

Store your seed in a cool, dry place. Most bird food deteriorates after a season or two, so don't store too much at one time. For good reason, birds will shun seed that's gone bad. How do you know if birdseed has turned bad? If you see mold on the seed, that's one indication. The other way is to trust your nose—if the seed smells crisp and nutty, it's okay; if it smells musty, throw it out.

There is, perhaps, one more piece of equipment you'll want to enhance your enjoyment of birdfeeding: a field guide. There are several good ones available. Probably the best way to choose is to wander into a bookstore and browse. Don't necessarily buy the most comprehensive guide; buy the one that will be the easiest and most fun to use.

Birdfeeding is not as equipment oriented as other hobbies such as golf, flying, or ham radio. But you will want at least a minimum of equipment. Where to find bird supplies? Attracting wild birds is so popular that practically any hardware store will have enough to get you going. Specialty stores—stores devoted specifically to feeding wild birds—abound throughout the country. Most owners of wild bird stores and salespeople at bird catalog companies are extremely knowledgeable and helpful. Give them a chance and they'll reveal all sorts of secrets about feeding wild birds. Besides stores and catalogs, you might contact your local Audubon Society for leads on purchasing birding supplies.

ATTRACTING THE NEATER SPECIES

LET ME STATE this out front: if you *want* to attract flocks of finches, mourning doves, sparrows, and blackbirds, you will never have a clean yard. Never. Flocks of birds and neatness can't occupy the same place at the same time. Many birds travel in large groups and descend on your feeder like a busload of elementary-school children emptying into a restaurant for lunch. By definition, *flock* means "mess." Some time ago my wife and I took a trip to a place called Heron Island in the Great Barrier Reef. A beautiful island, Heron Island was so named because of its enormous population of herons (and mutton birds, and terns). Herons are beautiful, nobody can deny that—but put hundreds and hundreds and hundreds together and your perspective on these birds changes. To walk along the island required wearing a hat—and it wasn't because of the sun.

The first step toward the goal of birdfeeding without mess is to prevent large groups of birds from visiting your feeding at the same time. One way to achieve that goal is to coax your neighbor into participating in this wonderful hobby with the largest feeder he or she can buy.

But another way is to discourage birds that travel in flocks from visiting your feeder. This means employing the technique of selective attraction: attracting only those birds you want, the neat birds. This is the cornerstone of neat birdfeeding. It will make your yard healthier, and your spouse happier.

At the onset you'll have to make a key philosophical decision to stymie certain species in favor of others. For some people that goes against the grain of birdfeeding: all birds should have equal access to your feeder. Frankly, I think attracting only certain species is practical and enjoyable. You couldn't feed every bird in a ten-mile radius even if you wanted to; the cost of the seed would exceed your monthly mortgage. You might as well raise Alaskan huskies. Indeed, even the most ardent equal-opportunity bird feeder shoos away pigeons (and probably sparrows and starlings, too). As it turns out, many of the neater birds are the ones that you want at your feeder anyway, and many of the boisterous, untidy birds are those you don't care for.

Attracting the right birds should be viewed as a challenge, not a chore. The more successful you are at foiling dirty birds, the more opportunity you will have to enjoy the birds you really want to see. Not only will there be fewer messy birds at your feeder, but by limiting the birds you entice to your feeder, the longer the seed will last.

The following is a list of birds by neatness. It takes into account how these birds behave as individuals and in a group. Many of the birds in the "Messy" category travel in large groups, so that any encounter with them will create a mess. In a later section you'll find detailed information on the neatness factor of individual species. Whether a particular species is neat or messy depends not only on the behavior of that species, but on the design of your yard as well. This short list gives you a quick look at the birds; the species-specific information should be used to help plan for your unique circumstances.

NEAT BIRDS	SEMI-NEAT BIRDS	MESSY BIRDS
Woodpeckers	Cardinals	Goldfinches
Flickers	Wrens	Purple finches
Sapsuckers	Juncos	Rock doves
Blue jays	Mourning doves	Sparrows
Tufted titmice		Starlings
Purple martins		Crows
Hummingbirds		Grackles
Hawks		
Chickadees		
Nuthatches		
Orioles		
Mockingbirds		

What makes a bird neat, semi-neat, or messy? First, as I mentioned, birds that travel in flocks are automatically categorized as messy. Any gathering of more than four feathered friends at your feeder is going to make your yard look like Dennis the Menace spent the afternoon. A large quantity of birds is not quality. When was the last time you saw a single finch at your feeder?

The second element that makes a bird neat or messy is whether it takes its food away to eat. Most birds like to snack at the feeder, but certain birds will use your feeder as a take-out restaurant, hanging around just long enough to get what they want, but making their mess elsewhere. Bird droppings are at a minimum when birds stay at the feeder just long enough to make their selection and pick up their food. Seed shells and spilled seed are nonexistent because the birds take the shells away with the food! Take-out birds usually linger at the feeder for a half minute or so, examining what you've left for them before taking the seed of their choice. Because they only take one seed or nut at a time, they return many times an hour, making for an interesting show.

Blue jays are consistent take-out birds. And with the right seeds, chickadees and titmice can be conned into not eating while at your feeder. Birds that take out their food are among the neatest birds, and the best to attract to your feeder.

Several species simply don't care for the typical feeder fare and consequently don't leave any mess worth noticing. Hawks, purple martins, and hummingbirds fit this category. These are what I call "guaranteed neat" birds.

Some birds fidget a lot while they eat. They move their heads, wings, and feet, scattering seed. These birds, including finches, mourning doves, and sparrows, have a lot in common with human children learning to eat solid food for the first time. They simply cannot meet polite standards.

Rarely does any bird eat everything that's offered. Most birds will sift through a feeder filled with mixed seed, selecting one kind and tossing aside the rest. Oh, what a mess they make! That's why mixed seed is a choice to be avoided.

Finally, what a bird eats makes a difference. Certain seeds combined with certain birds make less mess than other seed and bird combinations. Using whole sunflower seed or mixed seed is guaranteed to create a mess at your feeder; however, using peanuts, thistle, or hulled sunflower seed in combination with the right feeder can give you virtually a mess-free yard. I'd like to spend the rest of this chapter talking about using seed to attract neat birds and discourage messy birds. The strategies I discuss in this chapter are meant to be used in tandem with the techniques developed later in the book.

But I want to talk about seed first, because it is the most powerful tool you have for birdfeeding without the mess.

First, what not to use. As I've said, whole sunflower seed is out. Consider it on your forbidden list. Not only do the hulls damage lawns, but whole sunflower attracts most messy birds.

Millet also is a messy seed. It spills out very easily from feeders and attracts many untidy birds. Thistle can be used to attract neat birds, but only in combination with the right feeder. Same goes for safflower. I'll talk more about how to set up these seeds later.

At the other extreme are whole peanuts. Blue jays, tufted titmice, and chickadees adore whole peanuts; cardinals will eat them when hungry; but finches, grackles, starlings, and pigeons won't give them a second glance. Not shelled peanuts, which many birds will consume, but whole peanuts, which most birds can't figure out how to eat. (Crows like whole peanuts, but by using the right combination of feeders and feeder locations, as discussed later, you can perplex crows enough to keep them away.) In fact, if there is one single solution to the birdfeeder-mess dilemma it is using whole peanuts.

Blue jays, titmice, and chickadees, among my favorite birds, will pop onto your feeder for a handful of moments, take away a peanut, then come back for another. Blue jays will take the peanuts away to a quiet perch; titmice and chickadees will usually alight on the nearest branch, where they will immediately get down to the business of cracking that nut. It's loads of fun just to watch them pick the nuts up in their beaks. If you mix peanuts with other, foreign nuts such as Brazil nuts, acorns, and hickory nuts, you'll get to see birds "think" about the nuts before selecting one. Although I don't recommend mixing birdseeds, it's okay to combine nuts.

You rarely get spillage with peanuts. They're too yummy, too large a source of food, to be wasted or missed. Sunflower seeds, on the other hand, are easier for birds to ignore. If you offer the peanuts on a platform feeder, make sure the squirrels can't get to them, or they'll all be gone in a flash and the poor birds will have none.

Some woodpeckers, including red-bellied and pileated, will eat whole nuts, too, especially in winter. Whole peanuts are really the perfect food for those of you who want to be able to use your yard for other activities.

The downside to using peanuts is that they are relatively expensive. But because you will be attracting fewer birds, the cost of using peanuts exclusively may about equal the cost of buying sunflower seed. On the plus side, peanuts can be bought just about anywhere. You might even experiment with using other nuts in shells to see what varieties of neat birds you attract. (Pistachio, Brazil, and macadamia nuts ought to give you a truly selective group of neat birds.)

Don't feel obligated to keep your feeder filled constantly, no matter what you've been told. In fact, it's probably a good idea to let your feeder empty every few days or once a week for a complete day. Having your feeding go bare for a full day reduces the quantity of birds that frequent your feeder, which goes a long way toward reducing the mess. Finches, sparrows, grackles, and other noisy birds will, once they find your feeder empty, find some other birdfeeder at which to dine. Blue jays, chickadees, tufted titmice, and woodpeckers are bound to return tomorrow when you refill the feeder. Although I have no biological evidence to prove this, years of observation make me believe that the less messy birds won't disappear from your yard if the feeder is emptied for a couple of days, while the ruder members of the bird kingdom will find some more promising place to snack.

Thistle has its pluses and minuses. On the one hand, thistle only attracts a small variety of birds: finches in particular, but also juncos, indigo buntings, redpolls, and pine siskins. The good news is that goldfinches love thistle; the not-so-good news is that house finches love the stuff, too. (House finches are among the messiest birds.) Thistle's advantage as a low-mess seed is that it's consumed entirely; there are no seed hulls to spill away. And if there is any spillage, juncos will eat the remainder from the ground. If you use thistle, here are some guidelines: fill your feeder only with thistle; don't mix it with other seed. Use a thistle feeder so that seed doesn't spill away. (Thistle feeders are specially designed to hold only thistle.) Plug all the feeder's holes except for one, an act that discourages flocks of birds. Silly putty or chicken wire work well. If the mess is still more than you want, put the feeder in the corner of your yard. Forget thistle socks—nylon-stocking-type feeders. Their spillage rate is too high.

One more note about thistle: squirrels really don't care for it.

Suet is every bird feeder's favorite food, especially in the winter. It's easy to set up and almost universally liked. Unfortunately, there's almost no way to turn suet into an absolutely no-mess food. Squirrels will tear apart anything in their way to get at it. Finches will peck at the suet as they eat it. Bits of suet will fleck away to the ground as the suet is consumed. Chickadees will peck at the suet for the seed inside (if you are using seed-filled suet). And it's sloppy stuff to handle: suet feeders quickly become coated with a fatty residue.

Still, if you want to feed birds suet, go ahead. You won't have a perfectly clean feeder area, but there are two steps you can take to lessen the mess. First, use suet only during the cooler months. The warmer the weather, the weaker the suet cake. Conversely, suet won't melt and is more resistant to breaking apart during winter. Second, put the suet inside a large, hollow dome, such as a deep squirrel baffle. I had a suet cake suspended from the inside of a GSP feeder—the only birds that got to the suet were woodpeckers. And that was the idea. The presence of a large hood over the suet discourages many birds from attempting to snack, allowing only those birds that like to eat while perching vertically or upside down, such as woodpeckers and nuthatches. This configuration generally allows only a couple of birds at a time to feast. It's certainly not messless, but this is one way to attract suet-loving birds without turning your yard into a lard landfill. Suet is going to attract a large variety of birds, including cardinals, finches, flickers, nuthatches, starlings, creepers, titmice, thrushes, warblers, cedar waxwings, woodpeckers, and wrens.

Commercially prepared suet is fine, but there isn't any reason you can't prepare your own. There's even an advantage to making your own suet: you can shape it into any form you want so that it doesn't drip or flake off. Beef and bacon fat and shortening are excellent bases for mixing with fruit, seeds, peanut butter, and cornbread to feed the birds. Make sure that the fats aren't spicy.

These days it's tough to get fresh suet from the butcher; fresh suet is the firm fat from the cavity of cattle carcasses. More likely, you'll have to render fatty meat parts to get suet. Ask your butcher for about two pounds of throwaway fat to use for making suet.

Chop the fat into small pieces and place it in a heavy pot with a cover. Add a half inch of water to the suet, cover the pot, and heat over medium heat. As the heat melts the fat, remove the lid and cook until the bubbling stops, stirring occasionally. Strain the fat through a screen or sieve into a bowl.

Safflower is a favorite of cardinals, and only cardinals and American sparrows really like this seed. Cardinals don't usually travel in large flocks, so bird droppings won't be a concern. Cardinals are ground-feeding birds and prefer platform feeders when eating at manmade structures. But when hungry, cardinals will eat from anything. Because cardinals aren't especially neat—they will toss seeds aside—I suggest using a double platform. You'll have to innovate a bit to put this together, but it will give you a bright, shining lawn. To make a double platform, mount a large seed catcher below a moderate-sized platform feeder on a pole. That will keep the spillage and droppings to a bearable level. Put a squirrel baffle beneath the feeder to keep cats from trying to pounce while the cardinals are distracted. Alternatively, cardinals will eat from just about anything when hungry enough (such as in the winter and spring), so filling any feeder with safflower might give you success. The Select-A-Bird feeder (available in stores and catalogs) is one option. Here's how it works: a set of balanced weights permits only the species weighing the exact amount of the weights to open the feeder "door" by alighting on the perch. Birds that weigh more, or less, than the selected amount can't get the door to open. The Select-A-Bird comes in a pole-mounted and a hanging variety: the pole-mounted version lets you put a seed catcher below the feeder.

Not all cardinals are attracted to safflower at the onset, so you may have to mix it with sunflower seed just at first. Resist the temptation to use sunflower seed, either with or without the shell, for the long term. You'll only end up with a big mess.

Corn, millet, and—I am repeating myself, but it's worth repeating—mixed seeds make a mess. Avoid them.

Resist the temptation to *directly* feed the ground-feeding birds such as juncos, red-winged blackbirds, mourning doves, cardinals, pheasants, towhees, larks, thrushes, and common flickers. The purpose of these birds, from your perspective, is to mop up any seed spillage that does occur. And even with the best-prepared messless feeder there will be some spillage. Don't seek out the ground-feeding birds; let them find you. In other words, think of these species as your cleaning crew.

LOW-MESS FOODS AND THE BIRDS THEY ATTRACT

Whole Peanuts

Blue jay	Tufted titmouse
Chickadee	Cardinal (when hungry)
Nuthatch	Grosbeak
Towhee	Blackbird
Scrub jay	Steller's jay

Safflower Seed

Cardinal	Chickadee
Titmouse	Mourning dove
Scrub jay	Steller's jay

Bugs

(I've included bugs as a source of food, not because I recommend populating your yard with insects, but because certain species of birds, once attracted to your home, will also help you keep insects down.)

Wren	Purple martin
Eastern bluebird	Scarlet tanager
Woodpeckers (all species)	Nuthatch
Chimney swift	Black phoebe
Northern oriole	Tree swallow
Barn swallow	Chickadee
Tufted titmouse	

Thistle

Goldfinch	House finch
Purple finch	Thrushes
Indigo bunting	Pine siskin
Junco	

Berries

Blackbird	Blue jay
Steller's jay	Goldfinch
Wren	Purple finch
Robin	Steller's jay
Scarlet tanager	Tufted titmouse
Cedar waxwing	

Cheese

Carolina wren	Scrub jay
Thrush	Tufted titmouse
White-throated sparrow	

Peanut Butter

(A good standby if you're out of everything else, but the birds are still hungry.)
Chickadee
Mourning dove
Woodpeckers (including most woodpeckers, yellow-bellied sapsuckers, and flickers)

Spaghetti

Robins (No kidding)

As you experiment, you'll discover that different birds prefer different food at various times of the year. Chickadees may shun suet in the summer but eat it voraciously in the winter. You may even find that birds in your region will eat unexpected foods. If they like what you serve, keep dishing the same stuff out. With experimentation and observation, you'll be able to attract neat birds and repel messy birds.

2

*Neatness Profiles of the
Most Familiar Wild Birds*

SOME PAGES EARLIER I grouped wild birds by neatness. While this list is valuable and correct, not every neat bird is neat all the time. Conversely, not every messy bird is messy all the time. For example, the wren, an ordinarily neat bird, can be considered messy when she makes a nest in your mailbox. A lone finch (admittedly you don't see them that way often) isn't a terrible slob.

Another fact about birds to keep in mind is that they aren't always predictable. Sure, particular species have clear behavioral characteristics, but don't expect all members of a species to behave identically. They won't. Part of the reason may have to do with the way you've organized your yard—the plants, the dangers (from a bird's-eye view), the other feeders nearby, and so forth. All these elements may change the way a bird behaves. The more you know about birds, however, the better you will be able to design a messless yard. Use the scorecard that accompanies each profile to determine for yourself whether that bird is neat or a blight on your yard.

HOW TO INTERPRET THE MESSINESS FACTOR FOR EACH SPECIES

0–6 points   **Super neat**
Terrific bird. You might even consider letting this species fly around the inside of your house.

7–12 points   **Somewhat messy, but not a complete slob**
This species requires picking up after from time to time, almost like a small child.

13–18   **Very messy**
The kind of bird that has no consideration for your furniture, your lawn, or the cost of scattered, wasted bird seed.

19+   **Hopelessly messy**
Had this species been human, it would have reveled in the aftermath of college fraternity parties.

BLACKBIRD

Blackbird loosely defines about ten species of North American birds—all in the same family (*Icteridae*) with orioles, bobolinks, and meadowlarks. What blackbirds have in common: males are predominantly black or iridescent, and blackbirds are omnivorous, eating grains, weed seeds, fruits, and insects. Like most generalist birds, they've adapted well to living in a world overrun with humans and have exploited new habitats and diets created by development.

Blackbirds are particularly known for their huge family gatherings. In the fall and winter, they may flock together in groups ranging from a few to over a million birds. Several blackbird species may mix together, and they in turn may be joined by starlings and robins. The blackbirds most commonly found at feeders are the red-winged blackbird, common grackle, and brown-headed cowbird. They often flock and roost together.

Red-winged Blackbird

The red-winged blackbird, a seven-to-nine-inch bird—a little smaller than a robin—lives throughout North America. Even inexperienced birders quickly identify males, medium-sized birds sporting black with yellow-rimmed red epaulets, although the scarlet is often concealed when the wing is folded. People easily mistake the brownish female redwing for a starling, but a more careful examination reveals two obvious identifying features: the shorter tail and white streaks among their brown feathers. The immature male is sooty brown, mottled, but has the red shoulder patch. Redwings live from coast to coast, from Alaska south through Canada to the West Indies and Costa Rica.

In the not-so-distant past, redwings lived in marshes, along bodies of water, and in wetlands, building their nests among cattails and in reed beds. As the first settlers began clearing land, the redwings spread out. Today redwings have branched out into pastures, fallow fields, and other lots where they find enough tall weeds to support their hanging nests. Aggressive, opportunistic, and gregarious, they travel and roost in large flocks and even nest in colonies.

Outside of breeding season, redwings gather in enormous flocks, scour the countryside for food by day, and rest in communal roosts at night. As the weather gets colder, flocks get larger, and they may be joined by blackbird relatives and starlings. In the South, these multi-species roosts sometimes contain a million or so birds. In the winter, redwings are less numerous in northern states, because many migrate to the warmer southern climes where they can easily satisfy their omnivorous eating habits with available seeds and insects.

In the summer, redwings feast on insects—mayflies, caterpillars, weevils, crickets, and insect larvae, and occasional snails or newts— the best high-protein food for their nestlings. They also eat seeds they find on the ground and some cultivated grain. Occasionally in the late summer and early fall, they damage southern rice crops, pulling up the sprouted plants and eating the soft grain. Generally their insect-eating good outweighs their crop-damaging bad.

In the winter, they'll visit feeding stations, unfortunately often in large, menacing flocks. A flock of redwings will take over a feeding station. Luckily they don't outstay their welcome, but may come three or four times a day to fill up on tasty offerings. Unlike shyer birds, they gobble down all they can eat during the visit instead of grabbing a bite and flying away to consume it. They like corn, sunflower seeds, oats, mixed seed, millet, nuts, hemp, cracked corn, suet, bakery crumbs, peanuts, dried fruit, apples, and cheese—just about anything you could consider putting at a feeder. They prefer ground feeders, but that won't keep them from attempting to scale a sunflower seed dispenser for a mouthful of seeds. They'll spill seed and chase away other species. Bribe them into staying away from the hanging feeders by providing a ground feeder with cracked corn far away from the other feeders. Let the feeder empty and wait for the flock to move onto more promising feeding grounds. In the summer, they'll thin out, if not disappear altogether from the feeding stations, because their tastes turn to insects, necessary for growing nestlings. But they'll continue to visit feeding stations that are convenient to nesting grounds.

Despite their exploitation of new foraging and wintering grounds, redwings often return to the productive and secluded wetlands to nest. They're among the first birds to begin springtime courtship, with males returning from southern wintering grounds to gather in a chosen territory and sing the days away. Within a few weeks, the females follow, and the males begin a visual display full of fanning wings and tails and flashing scarlet epaulets.

Males command nesting sites according to their dominance within the group, with the most dominant taking the best nesting sites. Naturally the females try to match up with the males with the best sites. Males vigorously defend the few yards surrounding their nests, although they're colonial nesters and other birds share the same reeds and trees. They'll continue to feed peacefully together. Redwings attack other animals that stumble into the territory, even if the animal is human.

The female selects a spot in the male's territory and begins nest building. She completes construction in about six days. Typically, female redwings suspend their nests between reed stalks about a foot above the water, but they'll also use sturdy-stemmed weeds like goldenrod in drier upland areas or even a flat tussock, tree, or shrub. Nests are cleverly constructed affairs, woven from strands of reed and grass, mortared with moss and mud, and lined with grass. The female lays three to five bluish-white eggs spotted with brown and purple. The female alone incubates the eggs. Nestlings hatch after about eleven days, and for ten days are fed a high-protein diet of insects—mayflies, caterpillars, weevils, grasshoppers, and crickets and probably anything else the parents can catch. The young birds fledge soon and have to move on so the parents can get on with the second brood. The pair remains mated throughout the season and may have a third brood if the weather is good.

The survival rate for the young redwings is low—almost half of them die. But that's common in the bird world, and the parents make up for the low survival rate by producing more birds. Each female raises two to four offspring each year.

BIRDMESS SCORE

Use this chart to determine for yourself whether this species is messy at *your* feeder. By scoring each bird you'll be able to better decide which birds to attract and which to deter.

Number of birds at one time:

Seed scattering :
(0=none 3=low 6=medium 9=high)

Poop producing :
(0=none 3=low 6=medium 9=high)

Other:
(feathers left behind; moving twigs around the yard;
0=none 3=low 6=medium 9=high)

Is this species accompanied by other species?
(0=no 6=yes)

TOTAL:

Brown-headed Cowbird

In less hectic times, the brown-headed cowbird was known as the buffalo bird because the seven-inch creature usually followed these great beasts, eating insects stirred up by their lumbering gait. The buffalo bird was pretty much constrained to the Great Plains where the buffalo roamed. As zealous hunters and cattlemen drove the buffalo out, the cowbird switched loyalties to cattle and began to accompany the domestic bovines, gradually moving East and to all parts of the country. Both the male and female sport a short sparrow-like bill, but the similarities stop there.

The male's brown head and black body immediately identify it as a cowbird, but the female is colored a gentle gray. In many bird species, the female's color helps camouflage her while she nests, but the female cowbird uses her protective coloring to stealthily lay her eggs in the nests of other birds who raise the young cowbird as their own. The habit has earned the cowbird much notoriety in the world of birders, and many folks resent the cowbird's abandonment of parental responsibility, although the effect of the behavior on populations of other birds is difficult to gauge. Some experts think the cowbird has a role in the decline of songbird species, a difficult theory to prove, since other experts estimate about three cowbirds survive to adulthood for every forty eggs laid.

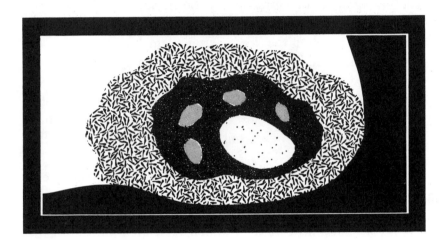

Cowbirds range coast to coast from southern Canada to northern Mexico, and the northernmost residents migrate to the central and southern states in the winter, leaving northern reaches by October or November and returning by March or April. Generally they stay south of Maryland, the Ohio Valley, and central California in the winter. Most of the year, they live in gregarious flocks of ten to several hundred individuals, often with redwings and grackles. They frequently roost and feed around farms, fields, barnyards, roadsides, edges, and river groves.

They eat mostly seeds and grains, with less than a quarter of the diet coming from insects. In the winter, they eat almost only seeds, usually weed seeds and waste grain. When they find a feeding station, they settle in and feed. Unlike some of the other blackbirds, they're not aggressive and pushy; they feed with juncos and sparrows. They're ground feeders and will eat just about anything you put out, except for fruit, which they won't touch. Once they show up at feeding stations, they stick around for a while to eat their fill. They'll probably settle in a roost near the feeder and return for daily visits.

At the birdfeeder, displays by male cowbirds—puffed-out feathers, raised wings, and bill tilts (beaks pointed up in the air) signal the beginning of courtship, the short time of year they don't live in large flocks. Males first establish their territories and then sing and display high in the trees to attract females. Once a female is attracted, the bond lasts throughout the season.

Cowbirds don't build nests but leave their eggs in the nests of gullible birds who incubate the eggs and raise the young as their own—at the expense of the host's nestlings. The cowbird nestling may usurp all the food or even push its adoptive siblings from the nest.

Cowbirds lay their eggs in just about any nest—150 different species' nests have been documented—but they don't always choose well. Cowbirds have been known to choose predator nests, and the cowbird nestlings don't survive birdlinghood. Other birds immediately recognize the brown-splotched cowbird egg and push it out of the nest, abandon the nest, or just build a new nest on top of the egg.

No one knows for sure why cowbirds so easily abandon their young, but the behavior may stem from their nomadic past when they followed buffalo around and would have had no time for rearing young.

Cowbird eggs hatch quickly, usually before those of the host species, and the nestling cowbird manages to do in the host's own young. It grows very quickly in a few days. Even though the nestling cowbird may be larger than its adoptive parents, the parents continue to feed it, packing extra food that would have gone to the host's nestlings down the cowbird's throat. As a fledgling, it follows the parents around for two or three weeks, begging food. Why the cowbird doesn't identify with the adoptive parents, no one knows.

BIRDMESS SCORE

Use this chart to determine for yourself whether this species is messy at *your* feeder. By scoring each bird you'll be able to better decide which birds to attract and which to deter.

Number of birds at one time:
Seed scattering :
(0=none 3=low 6=medium 9=high)
Poop producing :
(0=none 3=low 6=medium 9=high)
Other:
(feathers left behind; moving twigs around the yard;
0=none 3=low 6=medium 9=high)
Is this species accompanied by other species?
(0=no 6=yes)
TOTAL:

Common Grackle

The common grackle, a large bird eleven to thirteen inches long, sparkles in the sun. Their iridescent feathers make them easy to identify; the males sport iridescent purple on their heads and deep bronze or dull purple on their backs, while the females are less iridescent and a little smaller. Grackle comes from the Latin *graculus*, for the European jackdaw, a small crow, which early settlers recalled when they encountered the American bird.

Grackles live around farms, towns, groves, streams, woodlots, fields, and lawns in the U.S. and Canada. Larger grackles, like the boat-tailed grackle, found in the Midwest and South, and the great-tailed grackle, in the West, won't be taken for the much smaller, common one. They move in a generally southern direction in the winter, often in the company of redwings. They will roost with redwings, but prefer sites in upland deciduous or pine trees.

From time to time, people observe grackles rubbing ants over their feathers or even standing on an anthill and letting ants run all over their bodies. The behavior, called anting, is common in several birds but most often seen in grackles. No one knows quite why they do it, but many people suspect it's for skin conditioning. Grackles may also use other substances like mothballs or cigarette butts for anting.

The grackle lives in a variety of habitats although it evolved in the marshes with the rest of those in its family. In the spring, migrating grackles first return to wetlands where food is abundant—snails, insects, and other edible material. As the weather warms, they spread out to find food where they may, because they are generalized feeders.

Grackles live up to their reputation as feeder bullies; they've even been known to kill sparrows. Grackles love suet but eat any offering. If they can't feed on the ground, they'll attempt to get to the food in hanging feeders. They sometimes soak hard food in water—bread, crackers, or dog food—before eating it or feeding it to fledglings.

Like other blackbirds, grackles eat heavily from the meat side of the menu during nesting season, enjoying insects, fish, mice, nestlings, and eggs, and in winter they eat acorns, nuts, and tree fruits. In the springtime, they work hand in claw with farmers, following plows and eating cutworms, grubs, and other insects in freshly turned soil. Even though it appears they eat freshly sprouted crops, they're actually feeding on insects in the soil—a richer form of food for them than sprouted seeds.

They eat mostly insects in early summer, as well as minnows, salamanders, snails, mice, and goldfish from ornamental ponds; they spear or snatch up their prey like experienced herons. They'll also eat nestlings and eggs. They make up for that by eating more Japanese beetle grubs than any other bird. In July and August, they descend on grain fields to eat corn and wheat, and they feed here until winter, when they depend on weed seeds, waste grain, and animal matter. Grackles crack acorns in their powerful bills. They feed peacefully with starlings and robins, birds big enough to hold their own. Grackles engage in dominance displays with other grackles at the feeding station, using the bill tilt (with the bill tipped toward the sky for several seconds) observed in cowbirds, just to straighten out who's dominant in the group or to impress a potential mate.

Males attract females by singing a squeaky mating song delivered from tree perch or ground. Like other blackbirds, they enhance their serenade with a visual display, called a ruff out—outspread wings and tail, ruffed feathers, and dropped head to accentuate the iridescent feathers of the neck and back. Both males and females may ruff out, and alternate singing.

The mated pairs often build their nests in proximity to other grackles, most commonly in a grove of evergreens, but also in barns, natural cavities, orchards, deciduous trees, and, most dramatically, among the sticks of an osprey nest (ospreys feed on fish, not other birds). Nesting is somewhat colonial; several pairs nest in proximity. The grackle nest is a sturdy structure of twigs, grass, or seaweed, chinked with mud and lined with grass. Eggs are greenish-white to pale brown, blotched and streaked with dark brown. The female lays four to six eggs in a clutch. In some parts of the country both parents incubate the eggs, but west of the Alleghenies, only the female incubates. The nestling remains nestbound for two weeks and eats a high-protein diet of insects. When it fledges, it visits feeding sites with the parents, and learns appropriate foods. Grackles raise one brood a season.

 **BIRDMESS SCORE**

Use this chart to determine for yourself whether this species is messy at *your* feeder. By scoring each bird you'll be able to better decide which birds to attract and which to deter.

Number of birds at one time:

Seed scattering :

(0=none 3=low 6=medium 9=high)

Poop producing :

(0=none 3=low 6=medium 9=high)

Other:

(feathers left behind; moving twigs around the yard;

0=none 3=low 6=medium 9=high)

Is this species accompanied by other species?

(0=no 6=yes)

TOTAL:

BLUEBIRD

Despite the existence of many other blue birds, somehow the bluebird is the only one to go by so general a moniker. If it were to be given a more specific name, the blue thrush might be appropriate, for it's from the same family as the robin. Bluebirds molt once a year in the autumn as adults and are less brightly colored after molting. Most taxonomists agree there are three species of the bluebird: the eastern, western, and mountain bluebird, although the individuals from different species have interbred and raised young that breed with non-hybrid species.

The eastern bluebird is found throughout the eastern United States and in southern Canada. The adult male's dark blue back, head, wings, and tail contrast with a red patch on his breast and white belly. The female is less brightly colored—a slate gray on her back, head, wings, and tail with a red blush extending from her cheeks around to the front of her neck and down on her breast. Her belly is white. Both sexes have large dark eyes. Juveniles are brown or gray with white spots on the breast and flank and have a spotted breast like a juvenile robin. Some eastern bluebirds migrate to warmer climes in the winter, depending on individual preference and availability of local food. Because they don't follow traditional bird migration routes, we don't know too much about their movements during the winter. The ones that do travel seem to wander more than migrate; they drift to areas where food is abundant and the weather more to their liking. When they can find food, they spend the winter in the North.

Western bluebird males are a deep, sky blue on the head, back, chin, throat, wings, and tail. Red patches mix with the blue on the back, and the red moves along over onto the breast and flanks of the bird. The belly and undertail are white to blue-gray, depending on the time of year. The female is less brightly marked. Her head and back are gray, and her wings and tail are light blue. The breast and flanks are light red, and her belly and undertail are light gray. She has a white eye ring. The young western bluebirds are gray with a touch of blue on the wings and tail, but their white eye rings identify them as juvenile western bluebirds. Western bluebirds live in the western states and British Columbia, most abundantly along the California coast and in the Southwest, and they don't migrate much in the winter except to move down from colder, high elevations.

Male mountain bluebirds sport appropriate sky-blue feathers on their backs, and their breasts are blue instead of red. The female is not so bright; she's nearly totally gray or brown (depending on the time of year) except for under her wings and tail, where she hides some blue color. She has a white eye ring. Juveniles are brown to gray and sport the conspicuous white eye ring that helps identify them. Mountain bluebirds live in virtually all the western states and western Canada, from North Dakota to central Alaska. In the winter, they range further into the Southwest, into Texas and northern Mexico. The range overlap with the western bluebird allows for hybridization. Mountain bluebirds prefer the open land found at higher elevations, above 5,000 feet. Its habitat may be more treeless than that of the western or eastern bluebirds. It has more wanderlust than the other two bluebirds, too, and is often found in the East.

Although no one really knows why, bluebird populations declined in the twentieth century, probably because of habitat destruction and increased competition from the introduced starlings and house sparrows. The eastern bluebird has suffered the most; its population decreased by as much as ninety percent. As people became aware of the bluebird's plight, they began taking action by preserving habitat and providing nesting boxes for the bluebirds, secure nesting spots being key to their continued recovery. In 1978 bluebirds even gained formal human protectors: the North American Bluebird Society. Today bluebird populations are rebounding.

Bluebirds prefer open habitat with a few trees and low bushes around, suburban or rural habitats, farmland, cemeteries, and orchards, so it would seem that development has been good for them. Unfortunately it hasn't. While they're tolerant of humans, bluebirds are territorial towards other bluebirds in the summer, and that limits their population density on suitable land. They'll nest no closer than a hundred yards from another bluebird, with each pair commanding one or two acres of space. Because they prefer open spaces for hunting, perches with good visibility are important. The advent of the huge corporate farm with acre upon acre of crops without wooden fence posts, hedgerows, or windbreaks has spelled disaster for bluebirds because they lost all their convenient perches for hunting, holes for nesting, and lighting spots for fledglings.

They nest in natural cavities in trees, wooden posts, or even old woodpecker holes. Even though the world is short of the old-fashioned bluebird homes, today people erect bluebird nest boxes, built to bluebird specifications, for the birds to raise a family. Some bluebird guardians go a step further and actively discourage non-bluebird nesting in the box by destroying any attempts at nest building by house sparrows, starlings, or swallows. Bluebird houses are designed to discourage any but bluebirds settling in: the entrance hole is small to keep out starlings, and the house lacks a perch that would make it easy for house sparrows to set up housekeeping. Still, other birds find the houses attractive, and it's a battle to keep them out. Bluebirds overwintering in an area are grateful for the cozy bluebird houses for roosting, and as many as twenty may cram into the box for warmth.

Bluebirds act aggressively towards others of their species during mating season, but they're timid around other birds and are often bullied into leaving their territories. House sparrows and starlings, introduced in the late 1800s, began to crowd bluebirds around the turn of the century when they flocked to farms and open land. Some aggressive interlopers attack and kill bluebirds and their offspring or eggs and will build their nests right over a new bluebird nest, even if it has eggs in it.

Even if introduced species don't directly drive out the bluebird, they may force other natives into bluebird habitat, where they push out the gentle bluebird. For instance, house sparrows have driven some city-dwelling swallows out to the country, where they displace bluebirds from their nesting spots. However, swallows aren't as bad as they might seem, and many bluebirders allow the swallows to nest in one box and then erect another bluebird box five to fifteen feet away. Both species keep their own kind away but tolerate each other. Bluebirds hold their own against the swallow, and usurp swallow nests as often as swallows disturb theirs. Wrens, which inhabit dense woody areas, compete with bluebirds for nesting sites, and bluebird houses are best placed further than a hundred yards from dense thickets where wrens live.

Swallows and bluebirds make good neighbors because they both hunt insects; swallows on high and bluebirds on the ground. Open land interspersed with good perches like trees, shrubs, and fence posts is ideal for the bluebird. They perch and search. Once they spot an insect on the ground, they swoop down and grab it. They eat grasshoppers, crickets, spiders, ground beetles, and caterpillars, supplementing their diet with a little fruit. In the winter, they survive mostly on fruit and berries. During the spring, summer, and fall, eighty percent of their diet comes from insects. The rest comes from berries and fruit of plants like the dogwood, red cedar, sumac, bayberry, Virginia creeper, holly, blueberry, hackberry, and elderberry. Many people don't feed bluebirds directly but make food and water available to them.

Of course bluebirds hunt best in low grass, so if you want to feed bluebirds, keep the grass cut back to below waist height and make plenty of perches for them—leave dead branches, cut back leaves from limbs at about ten feet, or even sink stakes into the land. Plantings on your property can help attract bluebirds in both summer and winter. Look for berries and fruits with a high flesh-to-seed ratio because the bluebird has to swallow the entire fruit and can't digest the seeds.

Some people are successful in getting bluebirds to eat at feeders, although it's difficult. They'll eat suet, nutmeats, dried fruit (plump in boiling water first), and baked goods. A high-protein suet with dried fruit and peanut butter mixed in is attractive to them, too. They'll also eat mealworms, which you can buy at a pet supply store.

A platform feeder is an easy way to feed bluebirds, and you can get them used to the idea by beginning feeding on top of a bluebird box they're using for nesting. Or camouflage the feeder with sprigs of natural bluebird food like holly berries or dogwood fruit and place it near a feeding site. Birdfeeder manufacturers make special bluebird feeders, enclosed feeders with small entry holes that keep out larger species. Fill them with nuts, dried fruits, or mealworms. They'll also feed at a log drilled with holes and filled with suet. Bluebirds are neat feeders because they grab the food and run with it.

Bluebirds don't have fixed migration routes. Some make the trip south and some don't. They can overwinter just about anywhere, surviving on frozen berries from trees like the dogwood or on vines or shrubs. Some birders think feeding the birds encourages them to stay for the winter, but others point out that feeding may keep them from starving when freezing rain makes the berries inaccessible. They eat insects when the day is warm enough for insects to become active.

When individuals overwinter, the males are in a better position to claim the best mating territories in the spring. After the areas are claimed, the males sing from high perches to attract females. When the female arrives, the male sings softly and begins to point out all the potential nesting holes in the area until the female enters one. It can take several days to pick a nesting site. After they pick a nesting site, the male begins mate feeding, bringing food to his mate in the nesting site. Mate feeding begins with courtship and continues through nesting.

When the male isn't presenting the female with tidbits, they fly about their territory and keep in touch with calls and wing waves. The male follows the female closely and often leaves the nest box first. His close surveillance prevents her from mating with another and keeps her away from dangers like hawks. Studies show bluebirds may engage in extra-pair copulation, sometimes forming polygamous (one male attending two females) or polyandrous (two males attending one female) relationships. Pairs that raise a brood successfully in one year may stay together another year.

Over four or five days, the female alone builds the nest of grass, pine needles, and rootlets. When she is done, she nestles down in it to form a cup for the eggs, and then lays an egg a day until the clutch is complete. Bluebird eggs are very small and are a light blue to white. Sometimes a female will lay her egg in another bluebird nest and the adoptive mother will raise the young. Mountain bluebirds have biggest clutch—up to eight eggs, with an average size of four or five eggs. Eastern bluebirds lay from one to six eggs. Western bluebirds lay from five to six. All bluebirds usually have two broods in a season and can have three when weather is good.

Eggs hatch after about two weeks of incubation by the female (roughly the same for all species). The female is the only one that can incubate the eggs, and the male can only relieve her for short periods and brings her food while she sits. For the first few days after the eggs hatch, the female stays on the nest to keep the nearly naked babies warm. Then both parents begin feeding the babies insects and occasional berries, about two times an hour. Sometimes juvenile bluebirds from a first brood will help the parents feed the new nestlings. There are also cases where unrelated bluebirds, and even members of different species, help the parents feed the nestlings.

Nestlings are ready to fledge after about twenty days and their parents feed them for about another week. They instinctively know how to fly and head for the nearest perch. The second week they begin to learn to hunt by following the parents around, but they still get fed. After three weeks, they hunt on their own and get fed a little. By four or five weeks, the parents stop feeding them.

Mortality of fledglings is as high as fifty percent, and the bluebird can live about three years in the wild, ten years at the most.

PLANTS THAT BLUEBIRDS REALLY LIKE

American Holly	Autumn Olive
Bayberry	Bittersweet
Black Cherry	Blackberry or Raspberry
Blackhaw	Blueberry
Cascara Buckthorn	Chokeberry
Chokecherry	Cotoneaster
Crabapple	Dogwood
Elderberry	European Mountain Ash
Flowering Dogwood	Grape
Greenbriar	Hackberry
Hawthorn	Highbush Cranberry
Holly	Honeysuckle
Japanese Honeysuckle	Kousa Dogwood
Mistletoe	Moonseed
Mountain Ash	Multiflora Rose

Pin Cherry	Pokeweed
Pyracantha	Red Cedar
Red Mulberry	Russian Olive
Serviceberry	Snowberry
Sour Gum	Sumac
Viburnum	Virginia Creeper
Western Red Cedar	White Mulberry

 **BIRDMESS SCORE**

Use this chart to determine for yourself whether this species is messy at *your* feeder. By scoring each bird you'll be able to better decide which birds to attract and which to deter.

Number of birds at one time:

Seed scattering :
(0=none 3=low 6=medium 9=high)

Poop producing :
(0=none 3=low 6=medium 9=high)

Other:
(feathers left behind; moving twigs around the yard;
0=none 3=low 6=medium 9=high)

Is this species accompanied by other species?
(0=no 6=yes)

TOTAL:

BLUE JAY

Everyone knows this noisy blue bird with a crest. At eleven to twelve inches long, it's tough to miss the blue jay's appearance. A black necklace, black bars on its tail and wings, and bold white spots on its wings make a striking picture at any time of year. Males and females look alike. The blue jay ranges from southern Canada to Florida and migrates from Canada southward in the winter. It lives in oak and pine woods, suburbia, and towns.

Seven other jays are found in the U.S. The scrub jay is a western species, found in southern Washington south to California and east to Texas and also in central Florida. Scrub jays sport blue wings and tail, gray back and belly, and lack the crest of their eastern kin. The twelve-inch males and females look alike. The scrub jay is a common visitor to feeders in residential areas. It lives in open scrub areas and chaparrals of the West. In Florida, it shares habitat with the blue jay. The scrub jay is blue but has no crest or white patches on its wings or tail. Scrub jays hold many behaviors in common with blue jays and like them are omnivorous.

The Steller's jay is a common backyard jay found in the West. It's named for naturalist George Wilhelm Steller, who first identified the bird on Kayak Island in Alaska. Like the blue jay, it has a crest and is black and blue in color. The lower back, wings, and tail are dark blue while the head and shoulders are black. They have black barring on wings and tail. Steller's jays live in western pine forests, cleared areas, parks, and suburban areas, where they often eat at feeders. Hybrid Steller's and blue jays are found in Colorado.

The gray jay is a fluffy gray bird found in the northern boreal forests, preferring spruce and fir forests. Larger than the other jays, it ranges from eleven to thirteen inches. Gray (not blue!) on the wings, back, and tail and sporting a black cap with a white crown, chin, and belly, the gray jay looks a little like a chickadee on growth hormones. They're not found at feeders. Gray jays live from Alaska east through Canada and dip down into the northwestern U.S., the upper Midwest, and New England. Pinyon jays live in the Rockies and mountains of the far West. Green, gray-breasted, and brown jays are found in the far Southwest, along the Mexican border.

Blue jays evolved in woodlands and edges but today live in open areas of cities, towns, and suburbs. Omnivorous, aggressive, and intelligent, they're well adapted to live with humans. In general, populations shift southward in the winter, and blue jays spotted in the winter may not be the same individuals that live in the area during the summer. They are wary of being found in open areas. When they do migrate, it's in loose flocks of a dozen to two dozen birds. Before they actually migrate, however, they gather in huge numbers, around such points as Point Pelee in Ontario or Cape May, New Jersey. Blue jays are found most of the year throughout their range. By early fall, groups of juvenile and adult blue jays of many families gather, and they stay together in small flocks throughout the winter. The small flocks spend the winter together as they search for food and keep in touch with a constant chatter. These groups launch mass attacks on squirrels and hawks.

They're known for their raucous call, a screeching sound used in warning. (Their Latin name, *Cyanocitta Cristata*, is derived from Greek words meaning blue, chattering bird.) They use a number of calls, one of which approximates the call of the red-shouldered hawk. Blue jays also use a call to battle to invite other blue jays to gather forces, attack, and drive out owls and squirrels. They're not invincible, however, and are often dinner for larger birds of prey because they're relatively slow fliers, although they have a better ability to maneuver in forested areas and can escape a hawk there.

Blue jays are intelligent birds, and like other members of their family—the crow, raven, and magpie—are known to swipe bright, shiny objects and hide them. Like grackles, blue jays exhibit anting behavior: they can be seen rubbing ants over their feathers or letting

ants swarm over their bodies. Anting most commonly occurs during the late-summer molt, so perhaps it has something to do with skin care.

Blue jays sound the alarm when danger approaches in the form of a hawk, cat, or human, and all the other birds listen. Although they have a reputation for being bully birds, this is more a case of human interpretation. It's common in nature for smaller animals to make way for the larger ones, and when the foot-long blue jay approaches an area where finches, sparrows, or chickadees are feeding, it's natural for the birds to scatter.

Omnivorous blue jays eat just about anything that stands still long enough, but they're not as predatory on other birds as some people believe. A famous Audubon painting shows blue jays raiding a bird nest and feeding on the eggs, but that behavior proves to be exaggerated. A quarter of the diet is animal in origin. Animal protein comes from insects and occasional small fish, reptiles, and mice. They occasionally eat a nestling. Blue jays love nuts and are among the few birds that can handle a whole peanut, shelled or unshelled. They also enjoy acorns and corn and may carry acorns away and bury them to eat later. At the feeding station, they enjoy corn, sunflower seeds, and suet. They cram their gullets and mouths full of food and fly away to regurgitate it and eat it or bury it. They prefer flat feeders like ground or tray feeders, although they'll visit feeders with small perches. Several birds at a feeder will keep a distance from one another of about a foot, and any bird coming within that distance risks being attacked.

Yard plants also attract blue jays; they eat apples, berries, chokecherries, wild grapes, serviceberries, elderberries, hawthorns, pokeberries, sumac seeds, sorrel seeds, and palmetto seeds. They have strong bills that can open just about any nut, and they put their bills to many uses in food gathering.

The courtship is startling, with several males pursuing a single female. The entire group flies from tree to tree with the female in the lead, the males following, calling, and bobbing. For such a conspicuous bird, the blue jay is remarkably circumspect in its nesting habits. At nesting time, things settle down. The pair flies quietly around and often engages in mate feeding, when the male presents the female with a tidbit of food. The female receiving the seed or insect fluffs or flutters her feathers as she gives a soft call. The mated pair prefers a secluded, quiet nesting spot, usually in heavy cover. Both sexes cooperate to build a rough, bulky nest of sticks, often in an evergreen forest, but equally as often close to humans in heavily traveled areas. As humans alter their habitat, blue jays adapt to the changes and exploit the unusual nesting spots— flower pots or street lamps. The nests are about ten or twenty feet above the ground and are made of small sticks, bark, string, leaves, moss, and other available material, lined with soft twigs or roots. Jays may even usurp the nests of another, smaller species. Both parents incubate the eggs, a clutch of four or five olive-drab eggs with dark brown splotches. After three weeks, the eggs hatch.

Like most birds, baby blue jays hatch as helpless animals that must have every need attended. Not until the eighth or ninth day of life do the feathers begin to sprout from their sheaths, and they are ready to fledge at about three weeks. Baby blue jays are characteristically noisy, demanding food loudly. In the blue jay, parental care is extended, with parents sometimes feeding the fledglings throughout the summer. Unlike some birds, fledgling blue jays resemble their parents from their very first feathers. By the time the they're two months old, they're difficult to distinguish from adults.

Reports of blue jay attacks on humans are not exaggerated. Nesting jays protect their eggs with a fierce determination and will swoop down on innocent people merely hiking or walking near the nest.

BIRDMESS SCORE

Use this chart to determine for yourself whether this species is messy at *your* feeder. By scoring each bird you'll be able to better decide which birds to attract and which to deter.

Number of birds at one time:

Seed scattering :

(0=none 3=low 6=medium 9=high)

Poop producing :

(0=none 3=low 6=medium 9=high)

Other:

(feathers left behind; moving twigs around the yard;

0=none 3=low 6=medium 9=high)

Is this species accompanied by other species?

(0=no 6=yes)

TOTAL:

CARDINAL

The male cardinal is tough to miss: his bright red color, black throat and forehead, and medium size make him easy to identify. The female is a buff color with red on her crest, wings, and tail and a beauty herself. Both the male and female have red, short, strong beaks. Cardinals are a favorite with birders and non-birders alike, and probably anyone can identify the melodious red bird.

Cardinals sing throughout the year, while many birds only sing during the breeding season—and the female sings as well. Often a mated pair of cardinals will sing a duet, trading song phrases. People interpret the song differently: is it *What cheer! What cheer!* or *Birdie, birdie, birdie, cue, cue, cue, cue,* or *We-oo, we-oo, we-oo,* or *wheet, wheet, wheet?* The answer is, all of them. But you won't recognize a cardinal song everywhere you go. Parents teach the songs to their offspring, and the songs take on a regional flair so that birds in different parts of the country sing differently. One researcher documented sixteen song variations in South Carolina, another twenty-three in Delaware. They have a distinctive call, a pretty chirp, that's easy to recognize after you've heard it once.

With roots in South America, the cardinal is slowly migrating northward and westward. Their range extends from southern Ontario south to the Gulf states and West to Texas up to North Dakota. Cardinals prefer dense thickets with access to open areas: gardens, thickets, edges, orchards, roadsides, and wetlands. They seek areas rich in nuts, seeds, and fruits with plenty of secluded nesting spots. They're not migratory, and in more southerly areas, mated pairs and single birds spend the winter in small flocks near abundant food. Sometimes as many as fifty birds will gather together near plentiful food, but usually there are fewer. Cardinals are relative newcomers to the North, and they can survive the winter only if they can feed at birdfeeders. Like many birds that thrive under human development, the cardinal benefits from land-use patterns that create open areas bordered by forests and thickets. That and the numerous bird feeders that cater to the cardinal's tastes.

They enjoy different berries, grapes, dogwood fruit, Russian olive, sumac fruit—over a hundred kinds of fruit and seeds. Cardinals are early risers and are among the first visitors to the feeder in the morning. Like many birds, they love sunflower seeds and turn the seed in their mouths until they can crack it, then toss the shell on the ground and swallow the seed. Unfortunately they're messy eaters, and will toss aside filler seed to get to the tasty sunflower seeds contained in a mix. Cardinals are among the few birds that like hulled safflower seeds, and some people fill feeders with safflower to attract the cardinals. It cuts down on the mess, too. They'll also eat suet with nutmeats, cracked corn, melon and squash seeds, baked goods, and fresh fruit. Of course the neatest foods to feed cardinals are hulled sunflower and safflower seeds. Only about a quarter of their diet comes from animal matter. They'll eat a variety of insects, including locusts, beetles, and caterpillars, and will make sure their nestlings get plenty of protein.

Cardinals aren't always the most peaceful visitors to the birdfeeder. Sometimes aggressive individuals may drive others away while next door a different feeding station attracts several pairs of cardinals that feed in peace. In the winter, the male who so gently fed his mate through the summer may not even tolerate her feeding at the same feeder, especially if it contains a favorite food. They prefer tray or ground feeders, somewhere they can get firm footing. They're happy to feed from the seed catcher of some large birdfeeders, and they'll stay and eat until they get scared away. Cardinals are especially skittish and don't linger long at a feeder. They also tend to visit first thing in the morning and last thing in the evening.

In the spring, male cardinals begin their courtship. In the southern reaches of their range, they may begin as early as February and continue nesting as late as October, raising four broods. Males sing from the treetops and establish their territories, attacking competing males that dare intrude. Males also extend their crests as they sing to impress females, and they stretch themselves tall and thin. They become very aggressive; often in the spring people find cardinals attacking their reflections in car mirrors, windows, or other reflective surfaces. They think their reflection is an intruder and may spend hours trying to drive it off. Although the males are dominant at feeders the rest of the year, during courtship they are solicitous of their mates and feed them little tidbits of food. The pair also sings tuneful duets.

The female chooses the nesting site, usually in dense brush, and constructs a loose amalgamation of twigs, bark, and other materials. The cup-shaped nests are firmly attached to the branches that hold them, and they may be two to thirty feet above the ground. Look for cardinal nests among honeysuckle, roses, bayberries, and holly. The female lays three or four greenish-white, brown- and lilac-spotted eggs and incubates them alone—it would be too much of a risk for the eggs if the brightly colored male sat on the nest, although he may spell the female for brief periods. Eggs vary greatly in color, with some being nearly white and others nearly covered with dark markings. The male continues to feed his mate throughout nesting, and she sometimes sings to him from the nest.

Eggs hatch after about two weeks, and the female has to brood the newly hatched babies because, like all songbird young, they can't regulate their own body temperatures.

There have been interesting cases where two pairs of cardinals have picked the same nesting site and both end up using it. The females both laid eggs in the same nest, incubated them, and shared in the feeding of all the nestlings. Also cardinals have shared nesting sites—and parenting—with other species, helping feed nestlings of another species as the parents of that species help feed the cardinals. In other hard-to-believe cases, seemingly bereaved parents whose eggs didn't hatch may even help feed nestlings of another species.

Both parents feed the nestlings, making sure they get plenty of soft, easy-to-digest insects, feeding the growing birds as many as eight times an hour. After about ten days, the young cardinals fledge and may visit summer feeders with their parents, while the parents may gain back some of the weight they lost during the heavy feeding schedule. Juveniles resemble the female, but have black bills instead of a red one. They molt with the adults in the fall and soon are indistinguishable from their parents. To move things along, the male may take charge of the fledglings, helping them feed for as long as three weeks, while the female sets about incubating another batch of eggs. He shows them where to find seeds, introduces them to feeding stations, and teaches them how to catch insects. When the next clutch of eggs hatches, he has double duty, but by then the fledglings should be ready to take care of themselves. Cardinals have a long fledging period, and it may be a little over two months before they are completely independent. Cardinals don't venture far from their birthplace over their lives, and young cardinals usually settle near their parents.

BIRDMESS SCORE

Use this chart to determine for yourself whether this species is messy at *your* feeder. By scoring each bird you'll be able to better decide which birds to attract and which to deter.

Number of birds at one time:

Seed scattering :
(0=none 3=low 6=medium 9=high)

Poop producing :
(0=none 3=low 6=medium 9=high)

Other:
(feathers left behind; moving twigs around the yard;
0=none 3=low 6=medium 9=high)

Is this species accompanied by other species?
(0=no 6=yes)

TOTAL:

BLACK-CAPPED CHICKADEE

The chickadee is a plump, five-inch-long, common birdfeeder visitor. It's easily recognized because of its black cap, chin, white cheeks, and buff sides. The chickadee prefers the North and is resident from Alaska to Oregon, east through Canada and the northern U.S. to New England and the mid-Atlantic states. They live in woodlands, small groves, edges, gardens, and thickets where they can escape their enemies, raise families, and roost. It's named after its call, *chick-a-dee-dee-dee,* a whistle both sexes use to stay in constant touch with their kin when they're feeding out of sight. Chickadees have a lot of calls used for communication between a mated pair or among members of a winter flock. There are about ten representatives of the chickadee family in North America, only a few of which will cause confusion at a feeding station.

About a half inch smaller than the black-capped, the Carolina chickadee looks almost exactly like it, except that it lacks a white wing band and its tail is a little shorter. The Carolina chickadee ranges from Florida up to Maryland and west to Illinois and Texas, overlapping much of the black-capped chickadee's range in the mid-Atlantic states. Unless you can do a side-by-side comparison, it's tough to know which is which. The boreal chickadee, found in the far North, has a brown cap, black bib, and white cheeks, and won't be confused with the black-capped, nor will the western resident, the mountain chickadee, which has a white line over its eyes.

Most chickadees (except those in the far northern ranges) don't migrate south when the weather turns frightful, but remain in their summer range. The chickadee's inner coat of down and wind- and waterproof outer feathers keep the three-ounce birds toasty through cold winters. When they're not mated and raising families, they gather in small flocks of six to ten birds that control and defend a territory of about twenty acres. They flit around in edges and gardens feeding all day and then roost together at night in dense brush or cavities. Because they expend so much energy feeding and keeping warm on a winter's day, there's not much excess energy to keep them warm overnight. But some biologists suspect that at night they actually lower their body temperatures by about twenty degrees and slow their breathing and heart rates, actually awaking with a small energy surplus, enough to get them up and out in search of food.

In the winter they feed on wild fruit, nuts, and berries—especially poison ivy berries. Chickadees are particularly acrobatic and use their skills to capture insects quickly. They can feed upside down and cling to insubstantial leaves in search of food. In the summer, animal matter accounts for nearly all of the diet, but in the winter, the rate falls to fifty percent. They're great detectives and diligently investigate every square inch of a tree, from the bark to the fragile branches, for insects, their eggs, and larvae. In fact, they're such good winter hunters that the small chickadee flocks are sometimes accompanied by tufted titmice, downy woodpeckers, nuthatches, and brown creepers who want to benefit from the chickadee's talents. They also may want the additional protection from predators afforded by the alert chickadees. Their flying talents serve them well in evading predators, although not all chickadees manage to get away every time. They can turn and tumble quickly, easily swooping down into thickets or trees and under branches so those intent owls and bird-eating hawks can't keep up. Caught in the open, however, they are in serious trouble since they're not the fastest or strongest of fliers.

Chickadees eat sunflower seeds (hulled or in the shell, they like oil types first and striped second), shelled peanuts and peanut hearts, Niger, nutmeats, suet, and baked goods. They seem to prefer a hanging, swinging, unstable feeder—the types other birds will avoid. They eat quickly, grabbing a seed and flying to a branch to eat it, then waiting for another turn at the feeder. Because they've adapted to eating in all sorts of positions as they feed in trees, the suet feeders hung in a clear dome present no problem to them. They'll readily fly up in them, perch upside down, grab a bite, and leave. Their small flocks have strict hierarchical structure, and more dominant members feed first and displace lower-ranking members of the flock at the feeder. Bold, trusting birds, chickadees habituate to humans and will often feed near them; some patient birders have the tiny birds literally eating out of their hands. Once chickadees get used to a feeding station and people, they'll stay in nearby branches even when a human comes to fill the feeder, perhaps flying in to grab a fresh seed because they just can't wait to taste the new food.

When it comes time to mate, the two most dominant members of the flock pair off. The female initiates mate feeding by quivering her wings and calling *teeship teeship*. The male finds this irresistible and places food in her beak. It's the same behavior exhibited by hungry nestlings later in the season. Other than occasional mate feeding, chickadee mating is a quiet affair, and many pairs stay bonded year after year.

The male and female choose a nesting cavity, excavating a hole in old rotting stumps and dead trees themselves, or using an existing hole. If they have to excavate the rotting wood themselves, they're careful to spread beakfuls of the wood chips far from the nesting site so they don't give away the location. They may also choose an abandoned woodpecker hole or a birdhouse. Some folks line a birdhouse with wood chips to attract chickadees; the birds empty the site of the wood chips, and it seems to satisfy their home-building urge. The female builds the nest alone and lines it with soft material suitable for her fluffy nestlings. They prefer dense woods for their nests, places to protect the tiny birds and their eggs.

The eggs are so fragile that it's difficult for a human to touch them without breaking them. The female lays an egg a day for seven to ten days and then incubates the tiny, deep-red-spotted white eggs for about twelve or thirteen days. The male always stays nearby, feeding the female and protecting the nest from marauders like squirrels, snakes, and other birds who would like to eat the eggs. The female may leave for short periods but generally stays on the eggs until they hatch and then puts in an additional four days if the weather dictates, until the nestlings are capable of regulating their own temperatures. Chicks are hungry when they hatch, and the parents keep busy feeding them—sometimes as often as fourteen times an hour. After about two weeks the nestlings fledge, and after another two or three weeks they begin to follow the parents around, learning what and where to eat. The family may visit a summer feeding station and are especially attracted to suet. Despite the high-quality parental care, seventy percent of the young chickadees die, but nature makes up for that by having the chickadees nest twice in a breeding season. They also live longer than you might suspect. Naturalist Aldo Leopold captured the same banded bird for five consecutive winters, and some other naturalists have studied birds that are eleven to twelve years old.

BIRDMESS SCORE

Use this chart to determine for yourself whether this species is messy at *your* feeder. By scoring each bird you'll be able to better decide which birds to attract and which to deter.

Number of birds at one time:
Seed scattering :
(0=none 3=low 6=medium 9=high)
Poop producing :
(0=none 3=low 6=medium 9=high)
Other:
(feathers left behind; moving twigs around the yard;
0=none 3=low 6=medium 9=high)
Is this species accompanied by other species?
(0=no 6=yes)
TOTAL:

CROW

A close relative to the jays, ravens, jackdaws, and magpies, the American crow shares the familial trait of intelligence. Behavioral scientists find the crow to be pretty brainy. Some experiments have shown that they can learn to count to three or four, solve simple puzzles, and even associate symbols and noises with food. They can learn to mimic human speech, and through history have been favorite pets and companions for humans.

Crows dress in black from the tips of their bills to the bottoms of their feet, and the male and female look alike. They range all over the U.S. and live seasonally in Canada, heading South when the weather becomes too cold to bear. They live in open areas that provide trees for nesting and roosting and available food sources—around woodlands, farms, fields, river groves, and shorelines. As settlers developed land in North America, they created additional open habitat for crows, and their population grew. Despite poisoning, shooting, and even bombing, the species has continued to spread during the twentieth century. Crows gained protection under the Migratory Bird Treaty Act, and today, for the most part, live unmolested from suburbia to remote wilderness.

Cautious for such large birds (seventeen to twenty inches), crows are among the first to sound the alarm at the approach of danger. They examine an area warily before settling in to feed, and even then post sentries to protect them from enemies. When something alarms them, they sound the *cah cah* cry that puts all crows on wing. It's not that they're timid. In fact, a group of crows will attack owls and hawks until they drive them from the area. One crow sounds the call to assembly until a group forms, and then together the crows call harshly and dive at the predator until it flees with the crows in pursuit. They give up the harassment after ten or fifteen minutes, often only to start over again. Few bird predators are a match for crows, so it's difficult to understand why they drive all the predators away.

During the winter, crows gather in small family groups by day. Long before sunset these groups join other small groups as they all head for a common roosting spot. Hundreds or even thousands of these groups may gather until they reach the roosting spot, sometimes as far as fifty miles from the point of origin. The size of the roosting flock grows as the winter lengthens, and in some areas of the country, millions of crows gather. Maybe they just like the company of the other crows, but some naturalists think they gather for protection. In the morning they disperse, breaking up into smaller groups again.

During the fall and winter they feed together and occasionally run into other flocks at a feeding site. Then they're compelled to display and call until one of the groups gives up the site. Crows caw, bow their heads, wipe their beaks back and forth across a branch and flick their wings and tails until one of the groups give in, even if they're birds from the same nightly roost.

Crows eat plant and animal material, including carrion. About a third of their diet is animal in origin, mostly insects. Animal protein includes beetles, grasshoppers, caterpillars, crickets, spiders, millipedes, small crustaceans, reptiles, frogs, mammals, eggs, young birds, and carrion. They enjoy cultivated grain—corn and wheat—fruits, nuts, garbage, and scraps from the slaughterhouse. Some crows foraging near the water may gather shellfish and drop them to break them open. Just because they eat a wide variety of foods doesn't mean they can digest anything, as some people believe. Although crows will eat cultivated grains, farmers can use deterrents like repellents or scare tactics to protect seedlings and grain. Some even try offering alternative food, like cracked corn spread on the ground. Crows more than make up for what they eat by keeping insect pests at bay. Crows that live near heron colonies or waterfowl nesting sites may rely more on nestlings and eggs for food.

At the feeder, crows enjoy sunflower seed, peanuts, cracked corn, suet, and table scraps, especially meat. Crows are ground or table feeders and may gather in considerable numbers around a good food source. While some crows feed, others remain in the trees to stand watch; if your ground feeder is too close to cover, they might not stop at your station at all. They generally stay away from the hanging feeders meant for smaller birds, but may feed on the ground if there's spilled seed. In a day an adult crow may eat a pound and a half of food in about eight to ten small meals. A juvenile crow will eat half its weight in a day. Crows leave feeding stations to digest the meals, so at least they don't stay all day. Crows, like hawks and owls, cast up small pellets of indigestible matter such as bones, fur, scales, and hard seeds.

In the early spring, crows begin to pair off. The male courts the female with a song and display, and after he wins her, the pair may caress one another's heads with their beaks. They pick a secluded spot eighteen to sixty feet above the ground for a nest. The rough nest, constructed with twigs, sticks, and stems, hides a soft interior: grass, feathers, cloth, and string line it. They pick large pines, oaks, or even telephone poles as nesting spots. The female lays four to six greenish, brown-splotched eggs and incubates them for almost three weeks. Unlike many other birds, the male and female share in the incubation of the eggs. Crows generally have just one brood a year, although in the South they may have two if they get started with the first brood in February or March and the fall is mild. After five weeks the young birds fledge, and then stay with their parents for the rest of the summer. In the fall, the year's offspring form a small family group that in turn joins the huge flock of crows that congregate nightly for roosting.

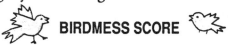 **BIRDMESS SCORE**

Use this chart to determine for yourself whether this species is messy at *your* feeder. By scoring each bird you'll be able to better decide which birds to attract and which to deter.

Number of birds at one time:

Seed scattering :

(0=none 3=low 6=medium 9=high)

Poop producing :

(0=none 3=low 6=medium 9=high)

Other:

(feathers left behind; moving twigs around the yard;

0=none 3=low 6=medium 9=high)

Is this species accompanied by other species?

(0=no 6=yes)

TOTAL:

FINCH

There are nineteen kinds of finch in North America. At the feeder you'll see the purple finch, house finch, goldfinch, evening grosbeak, pine siskin, and redpoll. Finches are small, seed-eating birds.

Purple Finch

Purple finches are really red, which makes them easy to confuse with the house finch. Purple finches, roughly the same size as a sparrow at about six inches long, have a red wash of color over their heads, back, and wings. The male's wings are striped, but not his sides, and he's white under his tail. You'll really need to study some pictures to learn the differences between purple and house finches. Immature males look like females, and it takes several seasons for the male to get his full adult coloration. Some males never attain full color although they breed and raise young. The female has distinctive facial markings: a white eyebrow and whisker marking enclosing a brown cheek like parentheses. Her chest is bright white with brown stripes. They're close relatives to the house finch and have similar behaviors as well as appearance.

Purple finches are resident in the northern U.S. from Maine west to Minnesota and on the west slopes of the Cascades and Coast ranges from British Columbia to Baja, California. Migrating purple finches may stop in the ranges of resident birds or continue southward to Florida, the Gulf states, the Great Plains, and the southwestern states, but the wintering grounds vary from year to year. They tend to wander south more than migrate, and they don't return to the same spot year after year as some other birds do. In the summer, many migrate into the northern coniferous or mixed forests of Newfoundland and northern Ontario west through Canada to British Columbia.

They especially like areas abutting open land: edges of swamps, streams, or logged areas, and in populated areas parks and cemeteries. They're shyer than house finches and won't live too close to humans.

Purple finches eat mostly seeds and soft fruits, except during the breeding season, when they may eat some soft caterpillars. Most of their diet—seventy-five percent—comes in the form of weed seeds, but they eat tree seeds as well: pine cones, and the seeds or fruits of the maple, birch, ash, mulberry, tupelo, and dogwood. At feeders, they prefer oil-type sunflower seeds but also eat thistle and canary seed. Purple finches prefer their feeders high off the ground and visit hanging feeders, second-story feeding trays, and platform feeders on a tall pole. Purple finches will feed with goldfinches and siskins at feeding stations and in natural feeding grounds. Perhaps the purple finch relies on these nervous birds to keep watch, as it feeds methodically and earnestly in an attempt to empty the feeder. Finches aren't what you'd consider to be carry-out birds.

Males may begin courtship singing from March to April, but they don't engage in serious courtship behavior until May. Then the males raise their crown feathers and dance before the females, sometimes launching into song and a flight. They seek nesting areas that provide tall conifers for nesting and the deciduous trees and shrubs that provide food. Purple finches build shallow cup nests high in the outer branches of trees, often conifers that conceal the nest well. They'll also nest in deciduous trees if the leaf cover is heavy enough to hide the nest. They breed from April to July.

The female builds a rough, deep cup and lays four or five green-blue eggs blotched with dark brown. She incubates the eggs for about two weeks, and the male brings her food. After the eggs hatch, both parents get busy collecting food for the young birds. Some of their first foods include caterpillars, cutworms, and other soft insects. The parents raise one brood a year, so after the young birds fledge and can care for themselves, the finches gather in flocks. Flocks feed together until time for migration, if the population is one that migrates, and then they all head south together. Otherwise they all remain together for the long winter.

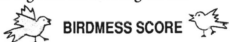 **BIRDMESS SCORE**

Use this chart to determine for yourself whether this species is messy at *your* feeder. By scoring each bird you'll be able to better decide which birds to attract and which to deter.

Number of birds at one time:
Seed scattering :
(0=none 3=low 6=medium 9=high)
Poop producing :
(0=none 3=low 6=medium 9=high)
Other:
(feathers left behind; moving twigs around the yard;
0=none 3=low 6=medium 9=high)
Is this species accompanied by other species?
(0=no 6=yes)
TOTAL:

House Finch

Until the 1940s, house finches were native to the West Coast, but then someone had the bright idea to import some to the East as captive songbirds. Authorities quickly cracked down on the illegal trade, and in the fracas, frightened pet store operators released the finches rather than be caught red-handed. The house finch set up housekeeping on Long Island and didn't spread much beyond New York through the 1960s. In the 1970s, they began to spread into southern New England, through the mid-Atlantic states, and down to the southern Atlantic coast. Now they've expanded into southern Ontario, south to Georgia, and they're heading West, currently stopped at the Mississippi River. They migrate south to the Gulf of Mexico come winter. In their native western range, they're non-migratory and breed up and down the West Coast, east to Texas and the Great Plains. In time, East will meet West in the mingling of the native western and introduced eastern house finch.

House finches adapted well to living around humans and their structures, as their name implies, but they also thrive in their natural environment in chaparral, old fields, and brushy deserts. They are adaptable and flexible birds, making the best of whatever circumstances come their way. They eat a variety of foods and nest in a number of circumstances. Wherever they live, they come in flocks unless it's breeding season.

The house finch is about the same size as the purple finch, about five and a half inches long. The house finch has less red on its head, back, and wings, and the male has stripes on his sides below his wings. The female has a bland face with no discernible pattern and dark stripes on her dirty-white chest. Considering their similarities, it's a wonder that competition between the species hasn't driven one of them towards extinction, but their preferences in habitat enable them to coexist, the house finch taking the city cousin role while the purple finch stays in less-populated areas.

House finches eat just a few insects during the breeding season, but generally they stick to a vegetarian diet. They often feed on weed seeds, probably more than half the time, but also they relish cultivated fruits, to the dismay of farmers. Different berries substitute for water in dry seasons and so are important to the finch, but the berry season is short. Most of the year, the house finch roams in flocks eating weed seeds available in open areas and along roadsides. In the winter, they're happy to find feeders.

At the feeding station, house finches eat just about anything in sight, a factor that must come into play in their amazing adaptation to life back East. They'll take suet, most seeds, bakery goods, table scraps, and fruit, but in the East, finches seem to prefer seed to other offerings. They like sunflower seed, thistle, white proso millet, and canary seed. They'll stay permanently in the area of a good feeding station and quickly become aggressive defenders of their food source. House finches drive off some smaller birds and the house sparrow to corner all the feeding station resources for themselves.

In the spring, house finch flocks begin breaking up into couples as the breeding season begins. The male sings his cheerful song throughout the day and from time to time struts around the female displaying his colored feathers. Once the bond is solid, they set about finding a suitable nesting site.

The house finch sometimes chooses a cavity for its nest site, nesting in holes found in houses, trees or nesting boxes, but most commonly they nest around human dwellings. They'll also build nests in deciduous or conifer trees, cactus, shrubs, vines, or even on the ground. House finch nests come in great variety; they're generally bulky structures built of any likely material the bird finds: string, bark, newspaper, fabric, hair, or grass. The gregarious house finch often nests close to others of its kind.

The female lays four to six pale green-blue eggs, speckled lightly with brown or black. After about two weeks, the eggs hatch, and the male feeds the female while she incubates the eggs. Like most nestlings, young house finches get insects to help them mature quickly, but mostly their parents bring sweet fruits and berries to them, a habit that makes the birds unpopular with fruit farmers. The birds fledge in about two weeks, and then the family joins up with large flocks and forages, sometimes causing damage to crops.

BIRDMESS SCORE

Use this chart to determine for yourself whether this species is messy at *your* feeder. By scoring each bird you'll be able to better decide which birds to attract and which to deter.

Number of birds at one time:

Seed scattering :

(0=none 3=low 6=medium 9=high)

Poop producing :

(0=none 3=low 6=medium 9=high)

Other:

(feathers left behind; moving twigs around the yard;

0=none 3=low 6=medium 9=high)

Is this species accompanied by other species?

(0=no 6=yes)

TOTAL:

American Goldfinch

The American goldfinch, also known as an elm sparrow because it feeds on elm seeds, is dispersed widely over the U.S. Some people also know it as the wild canary, because its melodious song resembles the canary's trilling notes. No matter what people call them, goldfinches are welcome backyard birds.

The male delights people who keep summer feeders; at that time, he's in his summer coloration, a bright yellow with a black cap and wings. During the rest of the year, the tiny goldfinch fades to a duller color, more like that of the female year-round. In the winter, it's virtually impossible to tell the male from the female by sight. The birds molt twice a year, a complete molt in the fall, and in the early spring a partial molt when the male dons his bright summer apparel and even the female sprouts barely noticeable yellow feathers on her breast. When they molt, the goldfinches grow an additional thousand feathers to keep them warm over the winter. They live for about three years in the wild. Bright coloration in males may serve a variety of functions for the wild birds, helping them defend territories or attract mates, but it also has nutritional benefits. People enjoy attracting beautiful birds to their feeders.

Goldfinches like open areas where they can find plenty of seed-bearing weeds. They evolved in wetlands, but today do well in a variety of habitats. Like many birds of the open lands, they benefited from development that created field from forest. Clearings attract goldfinches. They like overgrown farms, pastures, and orchards—virtually anywhere they can find thistle and other seed and suitable nesting material. In some parts of the country, part of the resident goldfinch population drifts southward in the winter while others remain behind. Most of the year, goldfinches live in small flocks and tend to roost singly.

As with the rest of the finch family, goldfinches are primarily seed eaters except when they're feeding nestlings. Then some of their diet may come from soft-bodied insects like aphids and caterpillars. Weed and tree seeds form the bulk of the diet for them. Goldfinch handily feed on what are problem plants to humans—dandelion and ragweed. In the winter, they generally switch their diet to tree seeds. They like seeds from the serviceberry, birch, hornbeam, sweet gum, mulberry, hemlock, elm, and alder. When they feed, they concentrate mightily, eating all the seeds available, and may not notice when people approach to observe.

They love Niger seed, and if you fill your feeder with it, they'll be sure to visit. Make sure the feeders are full before the goldfinches arrive in the spring so they'll find the food source early and return often. To keep other finches from the feeder, reduce the perches to a half inch in length so the larger birds can't perch there to feed. Thistle (Niger seed) is important to the goldfinch for more than food; they often line their nests with thistledown. Once they discover the Niger seed source, they'll return to the feeder often to eat. Goldfinches also eat hulled and unhulled sunflower seed, peanut hearts, millet, suet, and suet mixtures. Of all foods, they prefer oil-type sunflower seed. They use the hanging feeders well, but will visit ground feeders if they like the offerings. In the summer months, they also enjoy a clean birdbath and bathe and drink often.

Goldfinches are social birds, likely to visit feeders in groups of up to thirty. When they arrive to feed, they pull up a perch and proceed to eat their fill, much as they would on a flower head full of seeds. When eating wild food, they perch on a thistle head or in a birch tree and eat all the seeds they can reach before moving on, so when they visit feeders, the seed level drops noticeably.

Although courtship starts early, nesting for the goldfinch begins later, probably timed to coincide with the ripening of several types of wild seed the parents use to feed young birds. The long warbling songs characteristic of courtship begin long before breeding. Goldfinches remain in flocks even when courting, and males may join in song from high in the treetops. The females chirp and reply, and somehow males and females form relationships. The paired goldfinches wait until midsummer before seeking a nesting site, and they're one of the last birds of summer to nest. Then the sociable male goldfinches become territorial and fight to define and then defend their territories against their kind, although they'll tolerate other birds nesting nearby. Males protect the nesting tree and the immediate area but allow other males in the communal feeding areas used by all goldfinches. As the mating season progresses, the males become less territorial and don't mind so much when other goldfinches intrude.

The female picks the actual site for the nest, often on the very tip of a branch. Goldfinches prefer to nest in edges, hedges, shrubs, and the dense understory. The female designs a tightly woven, deep cup of fibrous plant material lined with thistledown, salsify seed tops, or other downy material. The goldfinch nest is so well constructed that it will hold water for several hours. Nests may be five to fifteen feet off the ground and are completed in about five days. The female rests for a few days and then lays five small, bluish eggs in the nest. Female goldfinches rarely have to leave the eggs to find food because their mates are so attentive.

After about twelve days of incubation by the female, the eggs hatch. The tiny birds are blind and featherless but develop quickly. They can see at three days and have their feathers after ten. Both parents feed the nestlings. Unlike many other bird species, goldfinch parents regurgitate partially digested food to feed the young rather than feeding soft insects. While the nestlings do get some animal material when they're fed, a large part of their diet is seed, so it helps that the tough seeds are partially digested when they get them. (The male feeds the female the same way when she is incubating eggs.) When the young fledge, the parents can feed them whole foods. And the parents continue to feed them for another several weeks. If the pair has time to raise another brood, the female will begin construction of a nest while the male continues to feed and teach the fledglings. By the time the new clutch of eggs hatches, the fledglings are on their own.

In the fall, the goldfinches gather into flocks for the winter, and they may feed with closely related birds, the redpoll and the pine siskin, which are similar in appearance to the goldfinch in their winter coloring.

BIRDMESS SCORE

Use this chart to determine for yourself whether this species is messy at *your* feeder. By scoring each bird you'll be able to better decide which birds to attract and which to deter.

Number of birds at one time:

Seed scattering :

(0=none 3=low 6=medium 9=high)

Poop producing :

(0=none 3=low 6=medium 9=high)

Other:

(feathers left behind; moving twigs around the yard;

0=none 3=low 6=medium 9=high)

Is this species accompanied by other species?

(0=no 6=yes)

TOTAL:

Evening Grosbeak

Not all that long ago, evening grosbeaks rarely visited suburban backyards; they stayed deep in the northwest forests. Evening grosbeaks prefer dense coniferous and mixed forests for both nesting and feeding, but perhaps they realized the vast opportunities available to seed-eating birds in populated areas and expanded their winter range. One of their favorite foods, the seeds of the box elder, are abundant in backyards, cemeteries, and other developed areas, and they like mature trees found in yards. Evening grosbeaks also enjoy sunflower seeds available at feeding stations, and perhaps that helped them expand their winter range.

Evening grosbeaks live year-round coast to coast along the U.S.-Canadian border, in the northwest U.S., and south into the mountain states. They winter south of the border into New England, the mid-Atlantic states, the Ohio Valley, and into the Plains states, sometimes going as far south as the Gulf states. The increased food supply available encourages the grosbeaks to venture farther and farther south and east.

Although the name would suggest the birds are active at night, they're not. You'll hear their musical notes from time to time as they feed during the day, but they sleep the night away like sensible birds. However, their thick, strong beaks match the French name they were first given; *grosbec*, or large bill. The shape and shade of the evening grosbeak's body bring to mind a goldfinch on steroids. It has a finch-like body shape, but it's about the size of a cowbird at eight inches long. The male evening grosbeak has a dark head with yellow, beetling eyebrows that meet just over its beak. The female is more subtly colored with just a touch of yellow but the same distinctive black and white wings of the male. Both male and female have a whitish to pale green bill that seems especially big and strong considering they eat many of the same foods their smaller relatives enjoy.

Evening grosbeaks eat many insects in the summer, but the majority of their diet is vegetable matter. Early in the spring, they eat tree buds and newly sprouted leaves, but they feed more heavily later in the season when they can get seeds. They're especially fond of the seeds from box elder, maple, and dogwood trees, and also eat seeds from the pine, spruce, fir, wild cherry, mountain ash, juniper, manzanita, Russian olive, hackberry, snowberry, and serviceberry. No seed is safe from their strong beaks, even cherry pits. In fact, they'll discard the sweet fruit to get to the kernel inside the cherry pit.

Evening grosbeaks forage in loose flocks among the treetops, hopping along the branches eating all they can reach. They're methodical feeders and not easily frightened. When food on high is scarce, they'll feed close to the ground on ragweed, sunflower, or other seeds. As summer turns to fall and then winter, the evening grosbeaks just gradually drift south in their search for food, and by December, flocks reach their wintering grounds. Some years grosbeaks arrive in hordes at the winter feeding grounds while in other years they're scarce in the same area. Their abundance or scarcity relates to the availability of natural food sources capable of supporting their flocks, and they may be absent from an area for several years.

When they come to a feeder, they come in numbers. They like high platform feeders or even hanging feeders, but a large flock will fight over resources and keep other birds away. To keep them happy spread the food over a wide area. They eat a lot, and they always come in flocks, so it's a great undertaking to feed them over the winter. But they may not come for another winter for quite a while, so why not enjoy them while they visit? Try feeding them hulled sunflower seeds, suet, safflower seeds, peanut hearts and meats, millet, cracked corn, fruit, and sometimes hummingbird nectar. Whatever you choose to feed them, be sure it comes hulled or the mob of voracious gourmandizers will litter the yard with empty shells. Try whole nuts like peanuts. Evening grosbeaks have a taste for salt and often feed on or near roads that have been salted for snow and ice. It's a dangerous practice, especially on hills and highways.

Anywhere between late March and early May the grosbeaks head north to their breeding range. Right before they leave, their beaks change color from yellow to pale green. If they stay late into the spring, the males may begin their mating songs before migration, offering a rare chance for people to hear their songs. The males also engage in mate feeding, a ritual in which a gallant male offers seeds to the female he's courting. It may take place at the feeder or in a nearby tree or shrub. Males or females may also quiver their wings and give short calls during mate feeding. Courting males awe the females with a quick dance in which they pivot back and forth with their wings spread. They breed from May until July. The female builds a shaggy, shallow cup nest of twigs high in a conifer tree, sometimes seventy feet up. Although a pair of grosbeaks will nest in sight of other mated pairs, they won't share their tree with others of their species. The female lays three or four blue-green eggs that are spotted with olive or brown.

After the young grosbeaks hatch, the parents feed them some soft insects, but then move them along to more conventional grosbeak fare, tree seeds.

 **BIRDMESS SCORE**

Use this chart to determine for yourself whether this species is messy at *your* feeder. By scoring each bird you'll be able to better decide which birds to attract and which to deter.

Number of birds at one time:
Seed scattering :
(0=none 3=low 6=medium 9=high)
Poop producing :
(0=none 3=low 6=medium 9=high)
Other:
(feathers left behind; moving twigs around the yard;
0=none 3=low 6=medium 9=high)
Is this species accompanied by other species?
(0=no 6=yes)
TOTAL:

Pine Siskin
Small, dusky-brown, striped pine siskins could be easily confused

with female house or purple finches, but the sharply pointed bill gives a good hint of their true identity. If you get a good look, you'll notice the small, five-inch bird sports a yellow badge on its wing and another on its notched tail. At one time or another, pine siskins visit most parts of the U.S. They winter irregularly in most of the eastern U.S. and live year-round in much of the western part of the country, Canadian British Columbia, and New England. Canadian breeding grounds stretch from coast to coast.

They're commonly in the company of the goldfinches and redpolls, the winter finches, each species staying in its own loose flock. It's easy to spot flying finches in the clear winter sky; they have uneven, undulating flight, each individual slightly out of sync with the others as they move through the sky. From the fall to early spring, siskin flocks number from dozens to hundreds. Pine siskins are vocal birds, and they call as they fly and become especially chatty when they land. They're morning singers, and often sound off from the treetops in late winter. During the day they forage together, sometimes damaging crops in the early spring.

Like the other finches, pine siskins are seed eaters. Early in the year, when the seeds aren't ripe, they'll eat buds and young leaves as they forage in the trees and shrubs, as well as young shoots from vegetable gardens, and flowers. They take occasional insects, especially during nesting season. When seeds become ripe, the siskins forage nervously among the treetops, feeding on pine cones as well as seeds from birch, alder, and eucalyptus. Siskins also feed close to the ground where they eat weed seeds.

At the feeder they take sunflower, melon, hemp, thistle, millet, and baked goods. They're tame around the feeder and eventually get used to people, but they're still nervous birds, constantly on the move even when feeding. They'll eat for a while, and then move around the area of the feeding station to check things out before returning to feed again. They'll use hanging feeders or feeding trays, but tend eat their fill before moving on, so try hulled sunflower seed and thistle to keep the mess down. Pine siskins love salt and often eat salt used to melt snow and ice from roads. They also have a taste for ash.

Pine siskins can be aggressive at the feeder. They give a head-forward threat to drive off other siskins, and species about their size and a little bigger. In a head-forward threat, they lean forward and open their bills toward the interloper with their wings raised slightly. Crowded feeders encourage aggressive displays, and before too long, a bird bigger than the pine siskin will come along to drive it away from the food.

In the springtime they move northward to their breeding grounds, but sometimes stay in the northern ranges of their wintering grounds to breed. The enormous flocks break up into smaller groups in the early spring when the members, perhaps thoroughly sick of one another, become aggressive and drive one another away. They're somewhat erratic in their nesting habits and breed sometime between March and August, often not returning to the previous year's breeding area. Courtship includes mate feeding, where the male feeds the female seeds, and aerial display accompanied by song.

The small groups become small nesting colonies. Mated pairs defend their own nesting area, but they continue to feed with the rest of the small siskin flock throughout the nesting season. The nests are usually at the forked end of an evergreen tree; they're shallow cups of twigs and bark that are densely lined with fur, hair, and plant down. The female lays and incubates three to six eggs, while the male brings her food. The small, blue-green eggs hatch after about two weeks. They raise one or two broods a year.

BIRDMESS SCORE

Use this chart to determine for yourself whether this species is messy at *your* feeder. By scoring each bird you'll be able to better decide which birds to attract and which to deter.

Number of birds at one time:

Seed scattering :

(0=none 3=low 6=medium 9=high)

Poop producing :

(0=none 3=low 6=medium 9=high)

Other:

(feathers left behind; moving twigs around the yard;

0=none 3=low 6=medium 9=high)

Is this species accompanied by other species?

(0=no 6=yes)

TOTAL:

Redpoll

Redpoll means redhead, *poll* being an old-fashioned term for head or the hair on the head, and the redpoll looks somewhat like a pine siskin with a bright red cap. Both the male and female sport the jaunty red cap, and they both have black chins, but only the male has a red wash over his breast. Redpolls breed in the far northern ranges of Canada, around the Arctic and sub-Arctic regions, and in Greenland, but they winter south throughout the northern half of the U.S. In fact, when they visit the U.S., it signals cold and snow and scarcity of food in the North. Historically, they've been moving farther and farther south each winter. In the far north, they feed on birch and alder seeds.

If they move South for the winter, they remain in flocks, often with goldfinches and pine siskins, and forage for tree seeds in the forest by day. It's not unusual to find them feeding low to the ground in open land like fields, gardens, or hedgerows. They can feed upside down perched on weed stalks, like the chickadee. They chatter noisily from the treetops during the day. They're tame and trusting and let people approach. Often they won't fly away from people but will just run through the grass. At night, they roost together in dense understory.

In the winter when we're most likely to see them, they feed almost exclusively on tree seeds, usually birch and alder, but in the summer, one quarter of their food is animal in origin. During the nesting season, they'll eat spiders, flies, ants, and some other insects. They also eat berries, pine seeds, elm seeds, and buds.

At the feeder, they eat Niger, hulled sunflower seeds, suet and suet mixtures, rolled oats, peanut butter, canary seed, and bread.

Male redpolls distinguish themselves by singing from heights during mating season. They may nest together in a loose colony. They build their nests low to the ground in Arctic and sub-Arctic tundra and in the trees in northern forests. They line them with ptarmigan feathers or plant down. The female lays five or six light blue eggs and incubates them for two weeks. The young fledge after about two weeks. The parents can only raise one brood during the short, northern summers.

BIRDMESS SCORE

Use this chart to determine for yourself whether this species is messy at *your* feeder. By scoring each bird you'll be able to better decide which birds to attract and which to deter.

Number of birds at one time:
Seed scattering :
(0=none 3=low 6=medium 9=high)
Poop producing :
(0=none 3=low 6=medium 9=high)
Other:
(feathers left behind; moving twigs around the yard;
0=none 3=low 6=medium 9=high)
Is this species accompanied by other species?
(0=no 6=yes)
TOTAL:

HAWK AND FALCON

It's not unusual to find hawks around feeding stations, although they're not interested in the offerings humans leave. They're there to prey on the birds. The sharp-shinned hawk eats mostly other birds; the cooper's and red-tailed hawks, kestrel, and merlin get about half their food by eating other birds. Hawks hunt by circling or perching on high and swooping down on the target birds.

Most prey birds know how to escape, so the hawks are no real threat to any species. Provide your bird visitors with plenty of escape routes—dense shrubbery or brush piles or tree stands where they can evade the hawks. Lest you consider taking things into your own hands, birds of prey are protected by law, so don't try to kill or harm them. Besides, their predation doesn't have much of an effect on songbird populations. Birds of prey have been feeding on songbirds since the days of feathery prehistory. Consider that the house sparrow is one of the kestrel's favorite foods and the hawks haven't really made a dent in the sparrow's population. Generally hawks cull the weak and diseased birds, which helps out nature.

Hawks are birds of the open country; generally they stick to fields, edges, parks, and roadsides where they can find lofty perches to use for hunting. Birds of prey frequent the edges of human populations, especially where they can find gardens that approximate woodland edges.

Many American falcons and hawks are cavity nesters and will use bird boxes. In foul weather, they'll roost in cavities too. Generally they lay three or fewer eggs, and they invest a lot of care in their young and raise one brood a year. Clues to a hawk's roosting spot: look for castings, undigestible fur, feathers, and bones they spit up and leave at the bases of the trees.

BIRDMESS SCORE

Use this chart to determine for yourself whether this species is messy at *your* feeder. By scoring each bird you'll be able to better decide which birds to attract and which to deter.

Number of birds at one time:
Seed scattering :
(0=none 3=low 6=medium 9=high)
Poop producing :
(0=none 3=low 6=medium 9=high)
Other:
(feathers left behind; moving twigs around the yard;
0=none 3=low 6=medium 9=high)
Is this species accompanied by other species?
(0=no 6=yes)
TOTAL:

HUMMINGBIRD

Hummingbirds are delightful little creatures that fill record books with their feats. The bee hummingbird, at two and a quarter inches, is the smallest bird. Hummingbirds have the most rapid wing beats of all birds—the ruby-throated hummingbird beats its wings seventy-five times a second. They get their names from the humming sound of their rapidly beating wings. Its heart keeps time too, beating 615 times a minute. All hummingbirds are magnificent fliers and can move backwards, forwards, and sideways—and they hover, too.

Most of the species of hummingbirds that breed in the U.S. are found in the West (shooting up through Canada and into Alaska), Southwest, and Pacific Northwest, but in the East, there's only the ruby-throated hummingbird. Common western species include the magnificent, rufous, blue-throated, Allen's, broad-billed, black-chinned, Costa's, Anna's, and Calliope hummingbird.

Most common to feeders are the ruby-throated, Anna's, rufous, and black-chinned hummingbirds—tiny birds that appear with a blur of wing beats accompanied by a slight hum. These birds appear in sunlight as a bright iridescent green (mostly the males; the females are often somewhat duller in color), but may seem black in the shade. The ruby-throated, of course, has a red throat; the rufous has a reddish-brown back and tail and scarlet-gold throat (depending on the light); the Anna's male has a bright red color at the crown and throat; the black-chinned hummingbird's black bib has a violet line beneath it. Hummingbirds represent one of the largest bird families, with over 320 different species, and most of those birds are found in South America. All hummers are at least partially migratory wherever they live, seeking warmer climes in the winter. They evolved in the heated environs of Central and South America, and they've not developed a taste for the cold.

Migrating hummers may take weeks or months to get where they're going because as they move, they're following blooming seasons of flowers. The small size of most hummingbirds belies their great strength. Their tiny wings are powerful on the up- as well as downbeat, while other birds rely on a powerful downbeat to fly. Hummingbird's elevator muscles are half as heavy as the strong depressor muscles that control the downstroke. In other birds, the elevator muscles may be a ninth as heavy.

Some hummers really put their wings to the test when they migrate. The ruby-throated hummingbird migrates an extraordinary distance each year, from various locations in the eastern U.S. across six hundred miles of the Gulf of Mexico to wintering grounds in Central America—and back in the spring. The tiny ruby-throated hummingbird gains up to two grams of fat in preparation for the flight, about half its body weight. It arrives in Central America two grams lighter. The rufous hummingbird breeds as far north as southern Alaska but still heads for Mexico in the winter, a two-thousand-mile trip.

Hummers live in open areas where they can find plenty of flowers. They're often on the move as the seasons change, because they can't get caught short of food. They're especially attracted to gardens, woodland openings, edges, areas along bodies of water, and shrubbery borders—mostly places where there are abundant flowers.

All hummingbirds are nectar eaters, consuming the sugary liquid found in flowers as well as some small insects and spiders. The high-energy food is essential to fuel the demanding lifestyle of the hummer. Not only do they need lots of juice to maintain their rapid flight, they also need to keep their internal body temperature warmed up to a high of 105 degrees Fahrenheit. Busily feeding hummers help pollinate flowers. They stick their heads into flowers and flick their tongues in and out to gather the sweet nectar, and sometimes their entire heads become yellow with pollen as they travel flower to flower. Somewhat sticky, their tongues also come into play for catching insects. They can catch flying insects on the wing or they pick them up around the flowers where they feed. Even though most hummers are small, they must consume twice their own weight each day because of their accelerated metabolisms. Relative to size, hummers eat more than any other bird.

Brightly colored flowers—red, pink, orange, and yellow—draw hummers. They've come to realize the rewards hidden in the brilliant flowers. Hummers can hover in front of the flowers as they feed and then dart left, right, up, and down, depending on where the next target flower is. Some hummers will land to walk and feed, but many can't walk and so hover and land when they want to change position. They like trumpet vine, shrubby and vining honeysuckles, day lilies, hollyhock, larkspur, lupine, bee balm, columbine, scarlet sage, red or rosy petunia, impatiens, perennial phlox, azalea, butterfly bush, Japanese honeysuckle, rose mallow, scarlet bush, and scores of others. Hummers are easy to feed, even if you can't attract them with flowers. Nectar feeders are small dispensers of a sugar solution the birds love.

Hang a nectar feeder near the plantings to get hummingbirds used to feeders and then gradually move it closer to the house where you can watch it. You don't have to dye the solution red since most of the feeders have red plastic on them anyway. Nectar feeders sometimes attract more than birds; insects like the sugar too. To discourage the ants, wasps, and other bugs who want to visit, hang the feeder with monofilament fishing line and rub Vaseline, salad oil, or mineral oil on the sides of the feeding tube so flying insects can't get a grip. Some people also put Vaseline on the fishing line. Hummers won't eat from an insect-covered feeder. Some people may think a honey-water solution would be more healthy than a refined sugar one. They're wrong. For one thing, honey solutions promote the growth of a tongue fungus in the hummingbird's mouth, one that can prevent it from feeding and ultimately kill it. Also, unlike some folks, hummers have the sense not to feed exclusively on junk food like sugar water, and seek out nutritious flower nectar and insects. In fact, when flowers are blooming in profusion, the birds may abandon the feeder altogether.

You can't find a neater eater than the hummer. While the feeders are some small trouble, requiring frequent syrup changes and a thorough scrubbing every few days, the feedees are trouble-free. They hover and suck the sugary syrup from the feeder, offering a thrilling show in exchange for pennies' worth of sugar. They don't spill syrup or leave unsightly bird droppings during their short visits (besides, how much mess can a third-of-an-ounce bird leave?)

Different species have different mating flights and habits to some extent, but they're all alike when it comes time to nest: the female raises the young hummers alone. A male attracts a mate with daring flight acrobatics; he flies high into the sky and then swoops down near the female. The patterns and rituals change somewhat from species to species. The courtship and bonding of the nuptial relationship lasts a long time, but in the end, the female raises the brood alone.

After they mate, the female lays two pea-sized eggs in her nest, a strong, stretchy affair constructed of spider webs, plant down, and saliva and camouflaged with lichen and moss on the outside. Hummingbird nests are so well constructed and hidden that there's little danger of the eggs or baby hummers being destroyed or eaten, so the female is secure in laying only two. Old nests are often refurbished the next season. For the common backyard hummers, the nests are usually no bigger than a golf ball, but they stretch to some extent to accommodate the growing hummer nestlings.

After two weeks of incubation, the hummers hatch, featherless and blind, resembling fat grubs more than birds. Mothers regurgitate meals into the mouths of the young, and poke their beaks so violently into the gaping mouths of the hungry nestlings that it's a miracle that the species even survives. She feeds them five times an hour. Hummers raise two broods a year.

 **BIRDMESS SCORE**

Use this chart to determine for yourself whether this species is messy at *your* feeder. By scoring each bird you'll be able to better decide which birds to attract and which to deter.

Number of birds at one time:

Seed scattering :
(0=none 3=low 6=medium 9=high)

Poop producing :
(0=none 3=low 6=medium 9=high)

Other:
(feathers left behind; moving twigs around the yard;
0=none 3=low 6=medium 9=high)

Is this species accompanied by other species?
(0=no 6=yes)

TOTAL:

JUNCO

Most people with feeding stations know juncos, tame, well-mannered birds. The slate-colored juncos have white nether parts. They're no bigger than a sparrow, about six and a half inches long, and have buff or pink bills. If the birds' feathers appear to contrast more sharply in the summer, that's just because their brown tips have worn away. Juveniles are naturally a browner shade than adults for the first two or three years of life, and the yearling birds' streaky-brown coloration proclaims their relationship to the sparrow family.

Often known as the snowbird, juncos appear all over the U.S. in the fall and winter and leave in the spring, when they return to their breeding grounds in the coniferous forests of the border states, Canada, and Alaska. They live permanently in the Pacific northwest, along the West coast, around the Great Lakes, and in New England and the Appalachians. In the winter, when they form small, gregarious flocks of about sixteen individuals, they can be found just about anywhere in the U.S. except for south Florida. Juncos are friendly with their kindred from the finch family, and are often in the company of sparrows and towhees. Juncos seem to be creatures of habit. Flocks tend to form with the same individuals year to year, and often the flocks return to the same wintering grounds repeatedly. Instead of huddling and waiting out a snowstorm, they seem to relish a flight in the snow, unless it's too much of a good thing. If the snow cover is especially heavy, the juncos venture further south in search of available food. Hence, in years with heavy snowfall, more juncos are found south of the snow line.

Not at all bold, juncos freeze rather than fly when danger is present. The group flies quickly to a tree and remains motionless. Their dark gray coloring serves them well, and rather large flocks go undetected in trees as long as they remain still in the darkness of the leaves. They're characteristically cautious when they travel, often traveling for short distances from tree to tree on the way to an objective. When they fly together, juncos are somewhat more confident. They roost together in their flocks, on the ground or in a tree, and as evening approaches the flock flies in unison, high, strong, and far, to the roost.

During the winter, birders often observe juncos in open areas, in edges, fields, parks, thickets, gardens, and along roads, but the breeding season takes them to northern forests, deciduous or coniferous, although they seem to prefer the latter. Since they feed in open areas, especially mowed fields and cut-over land, juncos adapt well to a variety of living situations and live well around people.

Mostly they feed on fallen seeds, picking up the visible ones and scratching for the ones below the debris on the surface. When they're breeding and must feed a nestful of hungry young birds, juncos increase the percentage of animal matter in the diet from a quarter to half of their food intake. They'll eat grasshoppers, ants, spiders, lacewings, caterpillars, beetles, and moths.

As confirmed ground feeders, juncos will rarely alight on low platform feeders, and certainly not on the hanging feeders meant for finches and small birds. They're not carry-out birds, but remain on the ground to eat their fill. That's not too much of a problem because they're so timid and may come and go several times in a day as they get frightened away from the feeder, gain courage, and return. An alarm call from one junco gets the whole flock on wing. Certainly they're not choosy about eating what the smaller birds may spill from the hanging feeders, and they enjoy a lot of the seeds that pickier eaters reject. Like the rest of the ground feeders, juncos serve a useful purpose at a feeding station when they clean up spilled seed. They eat millet, Niger, cracked corn, mixed seed, hulled sunflower seeds, peanut hearts, suet, baked goods, and peanut butter mixtures. Once they've found a good food source, they stay in the area to take advantage of the bounty, so the same flock may visit the feeding station daily. As the days lengthen, the birds know it's time to return to northern breeding grounds, and they'll abandon the southern feeding grounds of winter.

The birds only sing from early spring into midsummer, when they're mating. The male perches high in a tree and sends out the notes to attract females to the nesting territory, and the pair defends the territory during the breeding season. The cold doesn't seem to bother them, and juncos even nest on the summit of Mt. Washington in New Hampshire and elsewhere in other mountains above the timberline.

The nests are grassy assemblages, sometimes lined with animal hair or moss, built right on the ground or just a little off the ground, usually in dense brush, tangles of tree roots, overhangs on banks, or near an edge. The female lays four to six eggs that vary in color from whitish to greenish to bluish. They may also be spotted with brown or violet. Both males and females incubate the eggs, and after about twelve days, the eggs hatch. In another twelve days, the nestlings are ready to fly. Juncos raise two broods a year and build a new nest each time.

BIRDMESS SCORE

Use this chart to determine for yourself whether this species is messy at *your* feeder. By scoring each bird you'll be able to better decide which birds to attract and which to deter.

Number of birds at one time:
Seed scattering :
(0=none 3=low 6=medium 9=high)
Poop producing :
(0=none 3=low 6=medium 9=high)
Other:
(feathers left behind; moving twigs around the yard;
0=none 3=low 6=medium 9=high)
Is this species accompanied by other species?
(0=no 6=yes)
TOTAL:

MOCKINGBIRD

Once a firmly entrenched southern denizen, the mockingbird today lives throughout the country, excluding the far West and New England. In historical times, as recently as sixty years ago, they were rarely found in the North, though they are common there today. Plain, gray mockingbirds, with their long, probing beaks and attenuated tails, are among the easiest birds to identify. When they fly, mockingbirds flash their white patches to all below for ease of identification. Both sexes look alike and measure nine to eleven inches long.

They mimic the songs of other birds, animals, and even mechanical sounds they hear—rusty gates, sirens, and whistles. Their Latin name, *Mimus polyglottos*, means "many-tongued mimic." No two mockingbirds sing the same song, but each sings a complex tune, not repeating the same from day to day. Mockingbirds' singing abilities certainly gained the attention of colonists in the U.S., and in 1676 Thomas Glover in *An Account of Virginia* wrote, "As to the

Mocking-bird besides his own natural notes, which are many and pleasant, he imitateth all the birds in the woods, from whence he taketh his name; he singeth not only in the day but also at all hours of the night, on the tops of the chimneys." Their sweet song makes mockingbirds welcome in most yards, unless it's the early morning when males have been singing all night, vainly seeking a mate. It's not unusual for mate-seeking male mockingbirds to sing all through a spring night, especially during a full moon or near a bright street light. Only the male sings in the spring, although both sexes may sing the rest of the year.

Mockingbirds take to living near humans and do equally well in farm country, suburban towns, and cities. Once they lived at the forest's edge, but today they thrive around people and their development. We've provided cleared land, brush piles and hedges, and lovely shade and fruit trees. They're resident in many areas, but many mockingbirds migrate southward towards food when the weather gets cold.

Fruit forms about forty percent of the mockingbird diet overall. They eat fruits of the mulberry, holly, elderberry, pokeberry, blackberry, multiflora rose, grapes, red cedar, bayberry, and even poison ivy. They depend on the fruit hanging on limbs, preserved and cold, to get them through winter months. Mockingbirds that breed in the far north may move south when winter comes so they can get food. In the summer they eat insects, mostly catching them on the ground, but occasionally catching them on the wing. They love plumped raisins at a feeding station and also fresh fruit, oranges on a spike, suet and peanut butter mixtures, peanut hearts, nutmeats, baked goods, and hummingbird nectar. Since they visit singly and drive away competing birds, they're neat and pleasant enough feeding station visitors. Other fruit eaters, like the cardinal, bluebird, and oriole, will be easily intimidated by the aggressive mockingbird, but even the mockingbird can't be at all places at all times, so other visitors may be able to grab a bite.

Individual birds defend their feeding territories. A single mockingbird might control several backyards, and protects the area vigilantly against any intruders, often very apparently in the fall. What were once believed to be intricate mating dances are recognized today as intense territorial displays. Two birds face each other across the border, dancing hopping steps in one direction and then the other until one gives in and flees. Wing flashing, another behavior, may serve to drive away competitors. The mockingbirds flash their wing patches to advertise their dominance over an area. Sometimes wing flashing occurs when the mockingbird is alone and feeding on the ground. Then, some naturalists speculate, the mockingbird is scaring up insects by flashing the white patches. Their territorial dances are similar to the courtship dance, and it would be easy to mistake one for the other. Although humans have problems telling male from female mockingbirds, you would think the animals themselves would have no trouble. Yet the male seems to need behavioral clues. He responds aggressively during any encounter with another mockingbird, and if the reaction is submissive, he knows it's a female. Perhaps because they're somewhat more selective in their eating habits than other birds, their feeding territories are large.

Despite the fact that they won't eat the seeds at the feeding station (except for a rare hulled sunflower seed) the mockingbird may drive away hungry birds that wouldn't turn down a bit of Niger or millet. A feeding station in the mockingbird's territory and close to a prime fruit-bearing site threatens its food source, and the mockingbird will try to make sure no one gets in the area. Usually moving the feeding station halts the attacks.

Although the mockingbird's manners are rude, other birds often benefit from the vigilant gray bird. By driving off predators—pesky squirrels, snakes, crows, birds of prey, starlings, blue jays, and grackles—the mockingbird helps out the smaller, shyer birds. They'll attack house pets living in their territory, diving at dogs and cats, sometimes appearing to do it just for the thrill of it all. In nesting season, they'll even attack humans who venture too close to the nest. Although they rarely make contact, the dive is intimidating, and they may graze the head.

During the mating season in early spring, a male mockingbird sings loudly from the treetops, telling other males to stay away and advertising to all the females what a lovely territory he controls. He also performs aerial acrobatics, high, wide loops that expose the bird's characteristic white patches on the wing and tail.

The pair is fiercely protective of their nesting area, which is quite large—one or two acres or several backyards—and contains the food sources they rely on. They're alert to any sort of trespass. Unfortunate people, pets, and wild animals learn just how valiantly mockingbirds defend their breeding territory when the bird swoops down on a collision course with an intruder. If another mockingbird attempts to enter their territory, the males engage in a ritualistic dance at the border, each raising and lowering spread wings as they hop around until one gives up the area. Like the cardinal, they'll even attack their reflections.

After a very brief courtship, nest building commences. They nest in protected areas, in shrubbery and dense brush or even in climbing vines on human dwellings and outbuildings. They build ungainly, unwieldy nests in heavy cover like the thorny multiflora rose, about three to ten feet from the ground. Over four or five days, males and females build the nest together with a tough, thorny outer layer and a softer inner layer of leaves, twigs, moss, and hair. The female lays about four glossy eggs, blue to green in color and spotted brown. The female incubates the eggs for about twelve days, until the blind and featherless birds hatch. Both parents bring food to the young, soft insects to begin with and larger tougher ones like grasshoppers as the nestlings begin to grow their first brown feathers. After twelve days in the nest, the young birds are ready to fledge. The fledglings keep their brown coloration and spotted, dusky breasts until they molt in the fall. The juveniles disperse quickly and must define and defend their own territories as the parents turn to building a new nest and raising a second brood. The male may remain with the same female or they may find different mates for the second nesting. The mockingbird may raise two or even three broods between March and August, and at the end of the breeding season, even the mated pair turns against one another as they both establish separate winter feeding territories.

Mockingbirds, like all songbirds, have to be wary of their many enemies, cats, raccoons, skunks, opossums, and birds of prey. As with other songbirds, young mockingbirds have a mortality of seventy to eighty percent. By producing plenty of offspring, mockingbirds make sure the family continues.

BIRDMESS SCORE

Use this chart to determine for yourself whether this species is messy at *your* feeder. By scoring each bird you'll be able to better decide which birds to attract and which to deter.

Number of birds at one time:
Seed scattering :
(0=none 3=low 6=medium 9=high)
Poop producing :
(0=none 3=low 6=medium 9=high)
Other:
(feathers left behind; moving twigs around the yard;
0=none 3=low 6=medium 9=high)
Is this species accompanied by other species?
(0=no 6=yes)
TOTAL:

MOURNING DOVE

The mourning dove has fared much better in the company of humans than its close relative, the extinct passenger pigeon. They've been one of the more successful birds in adapting to settlement and today number around five hundred million. As with many other birds of the open lands, development has been good for the dove; they thrive in many different habitats, from open woods to farmland, to the mountains, and even into cities, where they may be found in the company of their larger relative, the pigeon, or rock dove. The mourning dove lives and breeds throughout the U.S., southern Canada, and up to Alaska, and nests in Mexico south to Panama. Other native doves, like the ringed turtle, white-winged, and common ground dove, are less familiar because they rarely visit feeding stations. Doves are related to Old World pigeons, very apparent when you watch them walk. Other songbirds may hop when they walk, but the dove places one foot in front of the other, head bobbing with each step. Mourning doves are a soft fawn color with black spots on the back, with pinkish feet and legs. When they fly, they display their white outer tail feathers. Males and females appear alike with subtle differences in coloration.

Quiet, shy, and unobtrusive visitors, doves don't give many clues that they've been in the yard—except for cleaned-up seed. Doves seek the quiet protection afforded by conifers, shrubs, and other plants, so bare, unprotected areas won't attract them. The birds spend a lot of time on the ground and enjoy basking in the sun with their heads tucked over their shoulders. Doves are sensitive to the cold, and some from the far north migrate to the South for the winter. During a harsh winter, all doves tend to migrate to warmer areas. In the colder parts of the country, doves gather in small flocks in the winter. They roost together, feed together, and maybe even migrate in the loosely formed social groups. Flocks of them will fill the sky as they fly towards feeding grounds.

Their swift, straight flight sometimes reaches sixty miles an hour, and the creatures are easy to identify at a distance by their pointed wings and tails. They flap continuously during flight, rarely gliding, often with as many as 147 wing beats in a minute. Usually they fly at a more relaxed pace of about forty miles an hour. They can suddenly change direction in flight, displaying more aerial skill than their bulky size would suggest possible. They're slow on the takeoff, however, and are vulnerable to cats and hawks when they're on the ground.

Hunters that might recoil at the idea of eating a robin or a cardinal relish the meat of these heavy birds, which may weigh 100 to 140 grams each. Many states, especially those in the South, support hunting seasons on the birds. At odds with hunters, animal lovers wish the bird with the meek personality no harm and appreciate the ground feeder who gladly cleans up what other birds spill.

Wild doves eat waste grain from fields, weed seeds, beechnuts, and small acorns. New harvesting methods and increased grain production helped the mourning dove population surge; they eat the waste grain the mechanical harvesters leave behind. In recent years, they've become familiar birds at feeding stations. The ground-feeding bird will fly to a platform feeder as well. They eat Niger, millet, sunflower seeds, safflower seeds, cracked corn, milo, nutmeats, peanuts, and peanut hearts. They also like lime, which females eat during early spring to help in egg production, and salt. About two percent of their diet comes from insects, snails, and other animal material. Dominant doves drive other doves away from choice feeding spots by raising and lowering their wings rapidly or running at the interloper with head and tail lowered.

Doves are somewhat more dependent on water than some other birds and always need access to fresh water. When doves come to feed, they're often in groups. The tendency is for one bird to feed at the platform while others clean up what's spilled on the ground, so they stick around while the eating's good. Mourning doves get a good rating as backyard bird visitors because they clean up messes left by other birds, and they have a live-and-let-live attitude that allows other birds to feed with them. They don't attempt to fly to hanging feeders where they'll spill seeds, and their flocks are small. They wouldn't be around your feeding station unless they found spilled seed on the ground. Doves fill their crops with large quantities of seed in a short feeding and then retire to cover to digest the seeds in peace and safety.

The mourning dove's woeful cooing earned it a memorable name, but the *coo-ah, coo, coo, coo* is the male's courting song, not an expression general malaise. In the springtime, the courting pairs bill and coo with apparent affection, earning them a reputation as loving birds. They perch near one another and the male bobs and coos at the female, following her as she moves around. During courtship, the male may perform aerial aerobics for the female. He soars high into the sky and then glides earthward with his wings set to perch next to the female. You may see him display his feathers and strut before her on the ground as well. Courtship may begin as early as February in warmer areas of the country, and the birds continue breeding until October if the weather permits.

Most birds feed and roost inside their nesting territory, but not the dove. The mated pair stakes out a nesting territory that will include the actual nest site, assorted perches, and places for gathering nesting material, but they feed and roost outside the nesting territory. Mourning doves will nest within sight of another dove nest, but they won't really associate closely, as some other birds would. The male picks a nesting site and even helps build the nest. They build a fragile platform of twigs, often on the ground, but more often about ten or twenty feet above ground level on a horizontal tree branch. If it's built in a tree, the eggs often show through the bottom of the scantily constructed nest because it's not lined. The female shapes the nest with her body, and the male often stands on her back while she's shaping it to give added weight to her efforts. Sometimes they even use an abandoned nest of a robin, mockingbird, or other bird as the foundation for the twig platform.

The fragile nests are easily destroyed by bad weather, and the flimsy construction contributes to the high mortality of the nestlings and eggs. In addition, the doves begin nesting early in the spring, before most other birds. Dove eggs and nestlings are easy meals for squirrels, cats, and predatory birds, easier meals than other species' nestlings and eggs because the doves aren't fierce defenders of their offspring. When the nest is threatened, the dove may feign an injury, trailing a wing upon the ground as if it's broken, to lure a predator away from the eggs or nestlings. Often they do nothing. Still, the mortality rate is in line with that of other songbirds; seventy-five percent of young doves don't live through the first year. Mourning doves commonly live about three years, although they may live until they're ten years old.

The female lays two white eggs and broods them for about two weeks, taking turns with the male. They each sit for long shifts, and the relieved partner leaves the nesting territory to roost and eat. As with most birds, the mourning doves are most active in the early morning and evening and spend afternoons resting and preening. Mourning doves are particularly dedicated brooders and rarely desert their nests. They'll even brood other species' eggs, seemingly unable to tell the difference between their white eggs and those of other birds.

Both parents care for the newly hatched nestlings, which are, like other newly hatched birds, featherless and blind. All bird nestlings have a difficult time thriving on a seed diet so the doves use an unusual strategy; they produce a crop milk, a glandular fluid produced in their crop. Crop milk is a nutritious food rich in protein (forty-six percent dry weight) and fat (twenty-six percent). Flamingos and emperor penguins feed their young a similar milk. The nestlings push their beaks inside the parents' open bills and drink the milk pumped out of the crop. The nestlings feed for about a minute at a time with brief rests until they are full—about six minutes. The feeding process is so labor-intensive that one parent can't do it alone, and if one of the parents dies, the nestlings die if they're younger than a week old. As the squabs grow, the parents gradually introduce seeds to their diet until they're eating seeds most of the time. The parents continue to brood their young until they are almost ready to fledge. When the squabs are about two weeks old, they fledge. The parents continue to look after the fledglings even as they begin the nesting cycle over again. Mourning doves may have two or more broods a year, and they'll use the same nest again and again if it proves successful the first time. In the South, doves may raise four or more broods each year.

BIRDMESS SCORE

Use this chart to determine for yourself whether this species is messy at *your* feeder. By scoring each bird you'll be able to better decide which birds to attract and which to deter.

Number of birds at one time:

Seed scattering :

(0=none 3=low 6=medium 9=high)

Poop producing :

(0=none 3=low 6=medium 9=high)

Other:

(feathers left behind; moving twigs around the yard;

0=none 3=low 6=medium 9=high)

Is this species accompanied by other species?

(0=no 6=yes)

TOTAL:

NUTHATCH

Its unique skill at climbing down a tree trunk headfirst earned the nuthatch the nickname of upside-down bird. While other trunk climbers like the woodpecker or chickadee go headfirst up the trunk, the nuthatch moves downward, finding all the edible goodies visible only to birds moving down the trunk. They're specially adapted for the climbing because where most birds have three forward-facing toes and one backward, the nuthatch has two facing forward and two backward. They spend most of their time on tree trunks and limbs, searching for food. Nuthatches get their name from the Old English word *nuthack*, for their habit of wedging nuts into crevices and using their beaks to hammer them open. Four types of nuthatches live in the U.S. Related to the chickadee, nuthatches have somewhat longer and more slender beaks, gray backs, and black or brown caps. Males generally are distinguished from females by their markedly darker head markings, but in southern areas there may be no discernible difference.

95

Red- and white-breasted nuthatches most commonly visit feeders, where they become so tame that they don't flee when humans come around to restock seeds. Both birds will learn to take seeds from your hand. The more numerous nuthatch, the white-breasted, lives in forest land throughout the U.S., preferring coniferous and mixed woods in the West and deciduous woods in the East. Redbreasts live in the coniferous forests of the north woods, down into the Appalachians, and in the West, often migrating southward during the winter. Their natural histories are similar, with only slightly different behaviors and food preferences. Both species visit mature strands of backyard trees. The two other North American nuthatches rarely visit feeders. The small brown-headed nuthatch lives in the southeastern U.S., and the pygmy nuthatch lives in pine lands of the West.

The white-breasted nuthatch is a six-inch bird with a black crown and nape, a dark back, and white underparts. The redbreast, at about four and a half inches long, is somewhat smaller. Its black cap, black stripe across the eye, and rust-colored breast make it easy to identify.

Mated pairs stay together year-round, living in twenty-five to forty-five acre ranges that may overlap somewhat with those of other pairs. In the winter, males and females stay in loose contact through the day and may roost separately or with a group of nuthatches at night. During the day they may form loose flocks, foraging with other nuthatches, chickadees, titmice, woodpeckers, warblers, creepers, and kinglets. White-breasts use their call to stay in contact as they move through woodlands year-round, but in the breeding season it may mean something else, because that's when they aggressively defend a small portion of their territory. When strange white-breasted nuthatches meet at overlapping boundaries, they adopt aggressive postures, give chase in flight, and sound rapid *yank, yank* calls until one gives up. The redbreast's call is different, but its territorial behavior is similar.

Redbreasts eat conifer seeds, insects, larvae, insect eggs, weed seeds, beechnuts, and Virginia creeper fruit. They may eat felled apples and sap from holes made by sapsuckers. White-breasts eat mostly the same food with a lesser dependence on conifer seeds because they frequent more deciduous forests. They eat insects, acorns, beech nuts, waste grains, and berries. Both forage for insects and other animal material as they move down the tree trunk; each bird can eat practically thousands of insect eggs. Sometimes they forage for nuts on the ground after they reach the base of the tree. Nuthatches like to store food under the loose bark of trees, where other animals find and consume it if the nuthatch doesn't hurry back. Still, the nuthatch probably evens the score by consuming nuts and seeds other birds and mammals store on the tree.

At feeders, nuthatches eat suet and suet mixtures, hulled sunflower seeds, peanuts and peanut hearts, melon seeds, nutmeats, baked goods, and occasionally nectar from hummingbird feeders. They'll eat from swinging hanging feeders and will drive away chickadees. The larger white-breast will drive off the smaller redbreast at the feeder, too. Usually a nuthatch will grab a seed or nut and take it away to eat nearby, but it may toss a dozen seeds to the ground before it finds the sunflower seed it's seeking, so mixed seed is a bad choice for them. When nuthatches eat suet, they may consume the food at the feeding station or fly off with it.

Sometimes as early as January the male nuthatch begins his courtship singing; breeding usually lasts from March to July. He ardently serenades the female, often bowing with each note, as she watches, seemingly enraptured. Occasionally she answers. Nuthatches mate for several seasons, which is probably the same as mating for life, two to three years on average. Males court the females most strenuously early in the relationship, but later, when the pair bond is strong, they may only sit close to one another, rubbing necks and bills during the early breeding season. They may also chase one another wildly, around tree trunks and tree to tree in short, mad chases that end suddenly as they begin eating or grooming nonchalantly. Later in the season, they engage in mate feeding, where the male presents tidbits of food to the female. The behavior may teach the male how to feed the young, a skill he'll need later in the season. If he presents a large insect, the female may refuse it until he beats it against the tree to tenderize it. Likewise, she may refuse the food unless he adopts a certain posture, as a parent feeding a nestling would behave. It's also good training for when the female is incubating the eggs and can't get food for herself. The couple continues mate feeding throughout the nesting season.

Nuthatches nest in tree cavities or birdhouses with the proper specifications. Nests may be anywhere in their territory, along a street or deep in the woods, high in a tree or close to the ground. They may use a hole excavated by a woodpecker or squirrel, a natural cavity, or in rare cases they may excavate rotten wood themselves. Nests are well-secured in the cavities and are often located at the bottom of a half-foot chute approached by an equally long entrance tunnel. The red-breasted nuthatch smears the entrance hole to the cavity with pitch, a habit that often gives it an unkempt appearance because it dirties itself going in and out of the nesting hole.

The male brings the female building material: bark, grass, twigs, and rootlets. The pair carefully lines the nest with soft feathers and fur, collected from animate and inanimate sources. Nuthatches often pluck fur from an unsuspecting living animal, but they are just as likely to take it from shed hair or a carcass. The female lays five to eight eggs, a large clutch because the pair usually only raises one brood each summer. The small, creamy-white, red-spotted eggs hatch after about two weeks. While the female sits on the eggs, the male brings food, sometimes as often as eighteen times in an hour.

Both parents care for the large family of hungry nestlings, bringing lots of food to fill their gaping mouths. The parents protect the nestlings from danger, often using a distraction display to perplex would-be predators. The nuthatch will cling to the side of the tree, extend its wings, and slowly sway from side to side, as if it's dying. The nestlings grow to fledgling stage in about two weeks, when they look exactly like small versions of their parents. Their best skill upon leaving the nest is climbing, not flying, and they quickly learn to hunt up and down the tree trunk, where they find caterpillars, beetles, flies, larvae, and eggs. After about a month, the fledglings are ready to declare independence and gradually drift out of their parents' territory.

BIRDMESS SCORE

Use this chart to determine for yourself whether this species is messy at *your* feeder. By scoring each bird you'll be able to better decide which birds to attract and which to deter.
Number of birds at one time:
Seed scattering :
(0=none 3=low 6=medium 9=high)
Poop producing :
(0=none 3=low 6=medium 9=high)
Other:
(feathers left behind; moving twigs around the yard;
0=none 3=low 6=medium 9=high)
Is this species accompanied by other species?
(0=no 6=yes)
TOTAL:

ORIOLE

When the settlers spread throughout the U.S., they gave new names to all the species they found there, often choosing names already in use in their home countries. Today, many names—the buzzard, the buffalo bird, the oriole—inaccurate as they are, remain in use and continue to confuse and dismay students of natural history. When English-speaking settlers arrived in North America, they immediately thought of the oriole of their faraway home when they saw this bright orange and black bird. The New World orioles belong to the blackbird family and aren't at all related to the Old World, true orioles that the colonists remembered. Several different species of what we call oriole live in North America.

The northern oriole breeds throughout the U.S., with the exception of the coastal southeast, and has become quite at home in suburban backyards. The orchard oriole lives only in the East but is equally at home with people. The Scott's, Altamira, Audubon's, and hooded orioles rarely visit feeding stations.

Northern Oriole

Beauty lovers everywhere appreciate the male northern oriole, a seven- to eight-inch bird with an orange breast and back and two-tone black and orange wings and tail. The female is less brightly colored, wearing an olive drab instead of black and rust instead of orange, and the juveniles appear the same. The northern oriole, claimed by national baseball today as the Baltimore oriole, was originally named for its bright orange and black coloration, the same colors used by the first Lord Baltimore for his livery and coat of arms. Until fairly recently, there was no northern oriole at all, only two different species: the Baltimore oriole in the East and the Bullock's oriole in the West.

With the sweep of a pen, the American Ornithologists' Union declared them to be the same species. Actually the birds interbreed where their territories overlap, and they do look alike. The Baltimore oriole has an all-black head, while the western oriole has a black crown and eye stripe with orange cheeks.

Northern orioles nest in most of southern Canada and the contiguous states except for some southeastern and Gulf states, but they usually winter in the warm Gulf states and south into Mexico and Central America. By early fall, the orioles make ready to migrate to warmer climates and gather in flocks to begin the trip. As they fly, they stay in contact by sounding their melodious call.

Plenty of stragglers remain during the winter around feeders in the Northeast. Wherever they're living, they seek out tall shade trees with light understory, usually bordered by open areas, and when they nest, they must have a stretch of open land or water on at least one side. Before the settlement of North America, oriole populations were limited by vast stretches of unsuitable habitat—prairies and heavy forests—but by planting tree windbreaks and shade trees in the grasslands and harvesting vast forests, humans opened up additional habitat for the birds. (Of course, forest-dwelling birds were less fortunate.) They've adapted well to suburban gardens, orchards, open woodland, and in the West, mesquite groves in desert washes. When they're not breeding, orioles may live individually or in small, loose flocks, usually of juveniles and females.

Most of their diet—about eighty percent—comes from animal matter foraged among the leaves where the orioles live. Insects are most important in the early to midsummer, but by late summer, they begin adding other material and searching for food beyond the leafy reaches of the trees. They'll eat soft fruits and berries—mulberries, cherries, some nuts, serviceberries, mountain ash fruit, and figs. But they don't neglect their vegetables and enjoy green peas. As the summer progresses into fall, orioles will also eat some seeds from flowers and vines. While fruit is easy to gather and abundant, it takes a lot of it to provide all the energy an oriole needs. Hungry orioles can do damage to cherry or other fruit trees in a short time, and they may become pests.

Frugivorous birds typically have short intestines and fruit may pass through the digestive system in as little as five minutes. So although fruit attracts some lovely birds, it may cause a different sort of mess than spilled food. Since orioles feed quickly and then move on, let's assume they're far away by the time they need to void.

At feeders they like nectar and oranges impaled on a stake, although they only seem to like them from the early spring until midsummer—probably because that's when they need to concentrate on catching insects for their nestlings. They'll also take chopped fruit, grapes, jellies, suet, peanut butter and suet mixtures, and hummingbird nectar, if they can find a way to perch. If you see orioles at your feeder in the winter, try feeding them raw ground beef instead of the baked goods, millet, or cracked corn you see them pecking, and they'll have a better chance of greeting their returning kin in the spring.

By early May all orioles have returned to their breeding territories, even the far northern ones. Males return first, claim trees, and wait a few days for the females to arrive. Orioles seem to especially prefer nesting in elm trees, but they also choose poplar, birch, cottonwood, pecan, and apple trees. Males sing robustly to protect their chosen trees, each male seemingly making his own song as he goes along, and then repeating it. When the females arrive, the males court them with dance and song. As the female watches, the male displays his feathers, bows his head, and sings a special courting song. When the pair finally makes a firm commitment, they choose a nest site.

They often choose a site above running water, a place safe from predation, but those sites go fast, so they'll also choose a spot overhanging an open field or street. The female builds a deep, gourd-shaped, woven nest hanging from a leafy branch anywhere between ten and sixty feet from the ground. Its tapering neck prevents nestlings from early ejection. She constructs it well with strips of bark, string, and weed stalk, weaving it tightly. She fills it with downy plant material or animal fur and then bounces inside the nest to shape it. An oriole nest takes a lot of work, and she finishes her labors in about six days.

Finally she can lay her four to six grayish eggs with dark brown or purple spots. After about two weeks the eggs hatch, and the nestlings remain in the nest for about two weeks more. The parents feed by regurgitation for the first few days, then move on to soft solid foods. Young orioles get a nutritious diet of mostly animal matter: caterpillars found in the trees, gypsy moth larvae, woodborers, and weevils. A few days after fledging, the young orioles are nearly independent, catching their own insects and feeding themselves. The male takes off for parts unknown and lives independently, although the female and juveniles remain together until the fall migration.

BIRDMESS SCORE

Use this chart to determine for yourself whether this species is messy at *your* feeder. By scoring each bird you'll be able to better decide which birds to attract and which to deter.

Number of birds at one time:

Seed scattering :

(0=none 3=low 6=medium 9=high)

Poop producing :

(0=none 3=low 6=medium 9=high)

Other:

(feathers left behind; moving twigs around the yard;

0=none 3=low 6=medium 9=high)

Is this species accompanied by other species?

(0=no 6=yes)

TOTAL:

Orchard Oriole

They're smaller than northern orioles and have a reddish-brown breast and black back. An inattentive observer might mistake the orchard oriole for the better-known northern oriole; they have similarly shaped, longish, sharp beaks and similar if darker coloration. The two share the same geographic range and live in the same habitat: orchards, small clumps of trees abutting open land or water, tree-lined streets, and shade trees in pastures. They tend to the warmer parts of their range, especially the Gulf states and the lower Mississippi where the northern oriole is scarce, and orchard orioles hardly ever overwinter in their breeding range, taking leave for Central America before the first breath of autumn. They migrate as soon as the young birds fledge and are independent, often by mid-July in the northern reaches of their range.

The orchard oriole eats more insects than the northern oriole. As much as ninety percent of its diet comes from animal matter. They'll also eat nectar, flower petals, stamens, mulberries, cherries, and blueberries when they're available. At the feeder, the oriole will eat a halved orange stuck on a spike, nectar from a hummingbird feeder if there's a perch, jellies, suet and suet mixtures, cracked corn, millet, and baked goods.

Orchard oriole mating is similar to that of the northern oriole. Juvenile males also go through the courtship movements, and some even manage to mate their first spring. The female lays four to six bluish eggs splotched with dark brown or purple, and she incubates them with occasional relief from the male, whose main role is to feed her. The eggs hatch after about two weeks, and the nestlings remain in the nest for another two weeks, completely dependent on their parents for food. They become independent quickly and are ready to migrate from even the most southerly reaches of their breeding range by August's end.

Orchard orioles often nest in loose colonies, frequently in fruit trees, where they build the characteristic hanging nest, but one not as long as the northern oriole's. They like to build them overhanging running water, but generally choose the tip of a tree branch over-hanging an open area.

 **BIRDMESS SCORE**

Use this chart to determine for yourself whether this species is messy at *your* feeder. By scoring each bird you'll be able to better decide which birds to attract and which to deter.

Number of birds at one time:
Seed scattering :
(0=none 3=low 6=medium 9=high)
Poop producing :
(0=none 3=low 6=medium 9=high)
Other:
(feathers left behind; moving twigs around the yard;
0=none 3=low 6=medium 9=high)
Is this species accompanied by other species?
(0=no 6=yes)
TOTAL:

PIGEON

Pigeons came to North America as early as the 1600s as domesticated birds bred from the European rock dove, destined to feed hungry settlers. As was inevitable, enough escaped the dinner plate to form a feral population, and they quickly adapted to open land everywhere: farm lands, parks, cities, and suburban gardens. Later in history, pigeons again became important when they were used to carry messages in both world wars.

Pigeons are larger than our native mourning dove and range in color from gray through pink to white with all sorts of patterns. The shy native North American pigeons, the red-billed of the Rio Grande Valley, the white-crowned of the Florida Keys, and the band-tailed of the West, rarely visit feeding stations. When people use the generic term *pigeon*, they inevitably mean the rock dove.

Perhaps more than any other bird, pigeons adapted to cities and thrive where other birds would perish. They nest on narrow ledges, eat just about anything, and produce young year-round, so there's no stopping them. Today people react with disgust at the thought of eating a pigeon—and often even at the idea of having pigeons eating and roosting nearby.

Pigeons didn't start out as bad birds, and they're not today, but their close association with humans makes them look bad. They started out on a healthy diet of wild and cultivated seeds and plants, but in cities they eat most edible by-products of civilization—including garbage and manure. When birds aren't breeding, they can survive on a poor diet for quite some time. Nature equipped the ungainly birds with large crops, so they can take in quantities of food to digest at leisure. The birds spend a lot of time just hanging out and digesting their meals. Where do they lounge? On our roofs, ledges, statues, porches, and trees, and in groups, too. As if the mere presence of pigeon droppings everywhere isn't bad enough, acid in pigeon waste can eat into building stone. And so while many people proudly feed the scorned pigeon, more people seek ways to discourage pigeon visitations to feeding stations.

They're ground feeders and usually won't even venture onto a small platform. Spilled seeds attract them and other ground feeders to stations, and often it's no real problem to have a pigeon visitor. Unfortunately they have a habit of moving in. Before folks know it, the pigeons feeding in the yard have begun roosting on the flat roof of the screened porch and building nests in the eaves. The pigeon droppings are everywhere.

Discourage pigeon roosting with Nixalite®, a sort of giant, spiny barbed wire that pricks birds attempting to roost on it. Try to increase the slope of their loafing spot to forty-five degrees or more so they can't comfortably hang out there anymore. Pigeons will be startled by bright lights, sudden noises, and raptor replicas, but they eventually get used to the stimulus. If the goal is to get rid of pigeons, the only recourse is exclusion since many states and localities forbid harming them.

It's tough to stop pigeons from visiting feeding stations. You'll have to clean up all spilled seed from the ground and perhaps even stop feeding for a few days as you shop for seed catchers and feeders that won't spill seeds. Pigeons usually won't fly to a platform feeder, so you can continue to attract finches, sparrows, chickadees, jays, juncos, woodpeckers, cardinals, mockingbirds, nuthatches, titmice, and wrens with a platform feeder raised one to three feet off the ground. Be sure to use a platform feeder with a high edge, or spilled seed will continue to rain upon the ground for the pigeons. They're inordinately fond of corn, wheat, buckwheat, white millet, and bakery goods.

Pigeon nests are messy structures, piles of sticks and grass on just about any flat surface, but especially surfaces up high. Rock doves evolved to live on high cliffs, so they like our tall city buildings. They may build no nest and just lay the eggs on a bare ledge. After about two weeks, the eggs hatch.

All bird nestlings have a difficult time thriving on a seed diet, so pigeons, like doves, produce a crop milk, a glandular fluid rich in protein (forty-six percent dry weight) and fat (twenty-six percent). The nestlings push their beaks inside the parents' open bills and drink the milk pumped out of the crop. They feed for about a minute at a time with brief rests until they are full—about six minutes. The feeding process is so labor-intensive that one parent can't do it alone. If one of the parents dies, the nestlings die, too, if they're less than a week old. As the squabs grow, the parents gradually introduce seeds to their diet until they're eating seeds most of the time. Juvenile pigeons grow quickly, and it's difficult to tell offspring from their parents. When the squabs are about two weeks old, they fledge. Pigeons breed most heavily in the summer months, although they nest year-round. Even as they're caring for the fledglings, the pigeons begin the nesting cycle again.

Pigeons seem to live longer than many birds, often as long as fifteen years. Urban birds probably have a tougher time of it with the dangers from cars and fast food diets. They may live three or four years.

BIRDMESS SCORE

Use this chart to determine for yourself whether this species is messy at *your* feeder. By scoring each bird you'll be able to better decide which birds to attract and which to deter.

Number of birds at one time:

Seed scattering :
(0=none 3=low 6=medium 9=high)

Poop producing :
(0=none 3=low 6=medium 9=high)

Other:
(feathers left behind; moving twigs around the yard;
0=none 3=low 6=medium 9=high)

Is this species accompanied by other species?
(0=no 6=yes)

TOTAL:

PURPLE MARTIN

Actually large swallows, purple martins don't need birdfeeders because they feed on insects. They're lovely birds, a dark black with purple highlights; the males are dark all over while the females and juveniles have light nether parts. They fly quickly on curved, thin wings as they gather insect prey. Martins maneuver well, can turn quickly to pursue, and can fly close to the ground, flapping their wings rapidly as they fly. Their forked tails help them steer so they don't crash into buildings and trees. They use a lot of energy going after insects, but they catch a lot of what they chase. Martins arrive early in the season because they're ready to go after the fast-flying insects of spring, not just the bumbling, clumsy summer fliers. They don't do well in bad weather and need plenty of insects to support their high-energy lifestyle. Martins control insects like mosquitoes that we consider to be pesky.

Purple martins breed throughout the contiguous states except for the Rockies and along the Mexican border, and they winter in South

America. They generally return to the same breeding area each year. They seek grassy open country, forest openings, bottomlands, open wetlands, and open land near water where they'll find plentiful insects.

You can do some things to attract martins. They do appreciate a bit of ground eggshell to help them produce strong eggs during nesting season, and they'll use martin houses erected for them, single models in the West and colonial apartment houses in the East. In the West, they'll use hanging gourds set out to serve wrens. Clean out the used nesting material annually.

SPARROW

There are dozens of native American sparrows plus an English cousin, actually a weaver finch, known as the English or house sparrow, a pushy chap who often drives out native species. You need a field guide in hand to identify all the different species, but they're all pretty distinctive. Five sparrows in addition to the house sparrow commonly visit feeders: the American tree sparrow, the song sparrow, the white-throated sparrow, the fox sparrow, and the white-crowned sparrow.

Most sparrows only winter in the U.S. and so become familiar visitors at feeding stations because they tend to return to the same wintering grounds every year. While the tree sparrows remain in large, peripatetic flocks of about fifty individuals, others, like the fox or song sparrow, remain alone or in loose flocks around the same area all winter. The male song sparrow may even remain in his breeding grounds if there is enough food.

At the feeding station, American sparrows prefer to feed on the ground close to easy cover for protection. The dense thicket is such good cover that the birds often remain deep within even when danger lurks without; they hop along the ground deeper into cover of the brush but won't fly out of it. They often scratch aside leaf litter and debris to find small seeds hidden beneath.

Sparrows will visit hanging feeders, but their feeding behavior of scratching is too firmly ingrained for them to be neat eaters, and they end up spilling a lot of seed on the ground. Sometimes it's easiest to bribe the sparrows to eat elsewhere by spreading seed on the ground in some far corner of the yard. Or fill feeders with seed they don't like. In the wild, they're all highly dependent on weed seeds and eat directly from the ground or perched in trees extracting seeds. Sometimes they bounce on weed heads to knock the seeds down to the ground where they can eat them.

American Tree Sparrow

The American tree sparrow has a reddish-brown cap, patterned black and brown wings, and a dark brown spot in the center of its plain whitish breast. It winters in the northern U.S., sometimes gathering in astounding numbers, but breeds in the northern tundra. There's some sexual segregation in the winter gatherings, and the female flocks tend to move further south than the male ones do. Tree sparrow flocks may associate with other sparrows, and often they're the most abundant species in the group.

The tree sparrow is another bird that doesn't match its name. It spends little of its time in trees. Instead it stays close to the ground in thickets, open woods, orchards, farmyards, gardens, weedy fields, marshes, and edges, where cover and food are plentiful. In the summer, it frequents the low bushes of the tundra. It's a cautious bird and flies to perch in bushes or trees whenever danger approaches, a behavior that probably led to its name. The tree sparrow moves by hopping around rather than walking.

Most of the time tree sparrows feed on the ground, scratching at the debris vigorously to uncover the seeds they eat. At other times, they perch on flower heads, eating the seeds there. In the summer, they eat some beetles, ants, grasshoppers, and other insects, but generally they stick to weed seeds like those of the ragweed, chickweed, and sunflower. When tree sparrows visit feeding stations, they choose food from the ground or low platform feeders, preferring millet and cracked corn to the sunflower seeds offered.

Generally they don't venture to the feeding stations until bad weather forces them there for food. Sparrows, like all the small seed eaters, have to peel and discard the husk from the seed kernel before they can eat it. They have strong, conical bills and well-developed muscles for crushing seeds. At the feeder, sparrows enjoy millet, sunflower seed (whole and hulled), fine-cracked corn, canary seed, safflower seed, Niger, peanuts, peanut butter, suet, and bakery goods. Because they migrate so far to breed each spring, tree sparrows need to add to their body fat over the winter, and their body weight actually increases over the winter when other birds are probably losing weight.

In March or April the American tree sparrow heads for its Arctic breeding grounds, where it remains until midsummer. Pairs form each spring, and they nest in low thickets and shrubs, often on the ground or just above it. They build a bulky nest of grasses, bark, and rootlets, lined with softer material like ptarmigan feathers, animal hair, or fur. The female lays four or five light green eggs and incubates them for about two weeks. After the nestlings fledge, the pair forages in the tundra as a family group until it's time for the September migration south, and they often return to the same wintering grounds they left seven months earlier.

Song Sparrow

At least the song sparrow lives up to its name with its lively, cheerful song. Song sparrows are resident to much of northern North

America, and they winter in the southern U.S. Migrating sparrows return to Canada each summer to breed. The song sparrow has heavily streaked underparts, a key feature that differentiates it from other sparrows. They live in heavy brush, often near water, and are likely residents of fencerows, open forest with dense undergrowth, and garden brush piles.

Song sparrows eat small weed and grass seeds in the fall and winter, but in the summer their tastes run to high-protein insects, which make up about half their diet then. During the winter, when they're dependent on seeds, they like to visit feeding stations where they can find millet, canary seed, and cracked corn. Like other sparrows, they prefer to eat on the ground, but will visit hanging feeders where they'll spill seed on the ground, often flying down to feed more comfortably there. The song sparrow enjoys water and often visits birdbaths to drink and bathe.

The song sparrow raises up to three broods a year between February and August. Often the first brood hatches in woven grass nests build in a weed patch on or near the ground. Subsequent nests are built higher up in shrubs, or they'll use nesting shelves built for them in outbuildings and walls.

White-throated Sparrow

The white-throated sparrow's white throat patch and black and white striped crown help identify it when it visits winter feeding stations in the East. White-throated sparrows breed in Canada but winter in the eastern U.S. from Kansas and Massachusetts to the Gulf. Like the song sparrows, they sing a lovely tune, often throughout the winter. The white-throated sparrow often associates with the Carolina wren over the winter.

They frequent dense brush where they find cover, roosting spots, and plentiful weed seeds on the ground for food. They're timid birds and seek cover in the brush whenever disturbed. At night, small flocks roost together in the brush, chirping noisily as they gather and settle in. You'll find them in tangled thickets, hedges, fence-rows, and brush piles in rural and town settings. In the spring, they often gather at the best sites before heading north to breed. In the brush, they hop about scratching the surface debris to find small seeds.

They need to fatten up in preparation for the summer breeding season, often a fifteen-hundred-mile trip, and then get enough food in the tundra to make the trip back again. They eat weed seeds, berries, and some insects in the summer. They'll feed on the fruits from the dogwood, elder, poison ivy, and alder. The white-throated sparrow rarely makes a mess by insisting on feeding at hanging feeders, preferring to stay on the ground or at low platform feeders. It eats peanut hearts, cracked corn, and chicken feed at the ground feeder.

The female weaves a nest from grass, bark, rootlets, and hair, often building directly on the ground in the thicket cover. She lays four or five greenish eggs and incubates them for about two weeks. The male helps feed the young for two weeks while they're in the nest, and then the fledglings begin to forage with their parents. They raise one brood a year. The white-throat migrates south in small flocks, often associating with juncos and other sparrows along the way.

Fox Sparrow

The fox sparrow, the largest and most distinctive sparrow with its red, fox-like coloration, lives most abundantly in the contiguous states; it breeds in evergreen forests from Alaska to Newfoundland and winters in the U.S. to southern California, the Gulf states, and central Florida. It winters irregularly, however, and may be abundant one year in the wintering range and scarce the next. The fox sparrow often hits the South in droves after a frigid northern cold snap. Not only is it abundant today, it's been around since prehistory; there are fox sparrow fossils dating from the Pleistocene.

Like the other American sparrows, fox sparrows are shy and reclusive, living in inaccessible, dense thickets, swampy areas, edges, fencerows, and garden thickets. When disturbed, they flee to thickets and trees. They feed mostly in open, grassy fields, hopping about to eat weed and grass seeds from the ground. The fox sparrow is perhaps the most enthusiastic scratcher of all its family. Using both feet at once and often jumping high into the air, it pushes aside leaves or litter in a flurried search for seed. Because of the energy they put into the food search and their especially long toes and claws, fox sparrows can even search through snow, allowing them to migrate to the summer range sometimes weeks before the other sparrows.

The female builds a large nest on the ground, or more rarely in a tree if there's a threat of snow, and lays four or five green, brown-spotted eggs. She incubates them for about two weeks. After the young birds fledge, they join the family in small flocks to prepare for migration. They remain in the small flocks throughout the winter.

White-crowned Sparrow

The white-crowned sparrow is easily identified by the striking white and black stripes on its crown as well as its distinctive orange beak. They're resident in the western parts of the U.S. but winter in the southern sections of the country. Many migrate to the northern reaches of Canada to breed in the summer. In the fall and winter, the white-crowned sparrow lives in tight flocks of twenty-five to fifty birds. Once the flocks form, they're closed. Individuals generally don't leave or join because the group controls a defined feeding territory, although they don't react aggressively when they encounter another flock. Within the group, there's some fighting over resources, and the regularity with which one individual displaces others indicates some sort of hierarchy.

In their breeding grounds, they like the small willows that abut waterways, but often in winter and in breeding season they live in dense thickets found around farms and towns. They run rapidly from a disturbance and dive into cover, where they feel safe. In the winter, the white-crowned associates with other sparrows.

This sparrow frequents feeders in the winter and fall, but in the spring and summer it adds many insects to its diet. Timid birds, they're easily driven away from feeding stations, where they feed on the ground. Unlike some of the other sparrows, they prefer peanut kernels and hulled sunflower seeds to white proso millet, oil and black-striped sunflower seeds, and cracked corn, which they'll eat in a pinch.

Like other sparrows, the white-crowned sparrow nests on or near the ground in dense thickets, but sometimes builds the nest high in an evergreen. The female lays four to five eggs, her only clutch of the season. They breed between April and August.

House Sparrow

The introduced house sparrow aggressively displaces many of our native birds, especially our sparrows, from both feeding and nesting sites. In 1850 the first house sparrows were released in Brooklyn, New York, and today they live and breed from coast to coast in nearly every habitat. Originally they did very well feeding on undigested oats in horse manure, but with the advent of the automobile, house sparrows found other food sources.

The house sparrow eats mostly plant matter with a few insects thrown in over the summer. Ground feeders, they scratch in the leaves like their American cousins to find weed and flower seeds. They eat almost anything at the feeding station and will alight on hanging feeders to get food, messily spilling seeds everywhere and driving other visitors away. Conventional wisdom says that the house sparrow won't bother a wobbly feeder, but don't you believe it; they get at anything. Generally they won't enter a small structure to feed, so that's one way to outsmart them. Another is to bribe them with a ground food source elsewhere. They like millet, baked goods, canary seed, and sunflower seeds. Perhaps you can attract a kestrel, which thrives on eating house sparrows.

House sparrows are cavity nesters, unlike their ground-nesting kin, and usurp nest boxes intended for wrens, chickadees, and purple martins. If the sparrows can't find a cavity, the females build their own bulky globular nest in a tree. It has several side entrances.

 **BIRDMESS SCORE**

Use this chart to determine for yourself whether this species is messy at *your* feeder. By scoring each bird you'll be able to better decide which birds to attract and which to deter.

Number of birds at one time:

Seed scattering :

(0=none 3=low 6=medium 9=high)

Poop producing :

(0=none 3=low 6=medium 9=high)

Other:

(feathers left behind; moving twigs around the yard;

0=none 3=low 6=medium 9=high)

Is this species accompanied by other species?

(0=no 6=yes)

TOTAL:

STARLING

Introduced in New York in the late 1800s, the starling has spread coast to coast. A misguided fan of William Shakespeare aspired to introduce to America all the species mentioned in the bard's works, so he got started by releasing sixty starlings into Central Park. Before long, they were breeding in the city and spreading west. They thrive in open areas afforded by human development, remaining resident year-round although they are migratory in their native Europe. Early on, they were migratory here as well, which helped them expand their range.

The starling's glossy, iridescent black coat changes to a white-spotted one in the winter, and its beak changes from yellow to black. Actually it only molts once a year, in the fall, but as the year wears on, the feathers wear out until all the white spots are gone. The starling's behaviors make it a bad neighbor. For starters, it flocks and roosts in huge numbers, often over a hundred thousand at once, and bird droppings cover everything, living or not, unlucky enough to be beneath the group. Just before sundown small flocks join other small flocks traveling to the final roosting destination, sometimes stopping to rest and be joined by other starlings. They chatter long into the night instead of going right to sleep. Huge starling flocks can decimate a fruit crop in no time at all, and aggressive starling pairs usurp the nesting spots of the smaller, more timid birds people prefer. You have to be awed at their cunning and expansionist zeal. In the fall and winter, starlings roost together, sometimes in the hundreds of thousands, in small tree groves or even sheltered buildings or bridges.

Starlings gather in huge flocks for most of the year, and even newly independent fledglings join the flock in the early summer. The flocks increase gradually over the summer, and by the end of the nesting season, they're huge. The flocks travel the countryside to forage on the ground, often accompanied by redwings, grackles, and cowbirds.

Starlings remain in flocks for feeding, sometimes descending on a likely food source and stripping it of all edible material before moving on. They love fruit, especially cultivated ones like cherries and apples, and can do great damage to crops. They try to make amends by eating copious amounts of insects they gather from fields and pastures, but no farmer really can forgive them. Half the starling's diet is animal matter; it eats pests like the cutworm, Japanese beetle larvae, and grasshoppers.

Despite their good insect-eating habits, starlings can be pests at the feeding station. They feed at ground and hanging feeders and scare off other birds because they're bigger and hungrier. When the starlings aren't breeding, they're not terribly aggressive, but their presence is enough to drive away small chickadees, titmice, and finches. They can invade feeding stations in huge flocks. Try distracting them to a far corner of the yard by putting cracked corn, millet, chicken feed, dog food, or cooked rice on the ground. They'll come to the feeders for any seed, corn, peanut hearts, peanuts, hulled oats, suet, table leftovers, and meaty scraps—just about anything you offer. They have a special weakness for suet, and the easiest way to discourage them from feeding on it is to position the suet so the starlings can't get to it. Protect the top and upper sides of the suet with a plastic dome so that only birds who hang upside down and sideways can get it, from the bottom.

When starlings switch from their summer insect diet to the fall/winter diet of seeds, their gizzards enlarge and their intestines lengthen to handle the fibrous material.

In more temperate parts of the country, starlings raise three or four broods a year. They begin searching for a likely cavity in early April and will remain in it throughout the breeding cycle. In crowded city conditions, starlings nest in loose colonies with others of its species along building ledges. Once a pair of starlings set their sights on a cavity, they usually get it, even if they have to drive other birds out. They're not too picky about the dimensions of nest boxes, and generally try anything they can fit into—a hole over an inch and a half in diameter. Plenty of folks with birdhouses spend their Saturdays and evenings in the spring destroying starling nests built in boxes meant for other, native birds.

When a male finds a cavity, he stakes it out, defending it from all who would enter. When a strange male starling approaches, the resident bird fluffs up his feathers and crows with his beak closed. The intruder wipes his bill on a branch and fluffs his feathers as well.

When a female approaches, he twirls his wings in the air and calls loudly to impress her. The female builds a bulky, soft nest of grass lined with soft material. She lays three to six greenish eggs and incubates them for about two weeks. Both parents feed the young, which are ready to fledge in about twelve days. Nestlings have big appetites, and their parents are hard pressed to bring them enough food, often feeding them throughout the daylight hours an average of once every six minutes. The young starlings eat mostly insects; ninety-five percent of the diet is animal matter.

 **BIRDMESS SCORE**

Use this chart to determine for yourself whether this species is messy at *your* feeder. By scoring each bird you'll be able to better decide which birds to attract and which to deter.
Number of birds at one time:
Seed scattering :
(0=none 3=low 6=medium 9=high)
Poop producing :
(0=none 3=low 6=medium 9=high)
Other:
(feathers left behind; moving twigs around the yard;
0=none 3=low 6=medium 9=high)
Is this species accompanied by other species?
(0=no 6=yes)
TOTAL:

TITMOUSE

Three titmice live in North America: the tufted in the East, and the bridled and the plain in the West. The tufted historically was a southern bird, but it's slowly making its way north and is today resident in the eastern U.S., while the plain titmouse is resident from California east into the southern mountain states, acting as the western counterpart to the tufted titmouse. The tufted titmouse is a small, gray, crested bird, enjoyed by birders because of its cheerful and energetic disposition. It lives in deciduous woods found in bottomlands, river groves, and swamps and in the shade trees in gardens and parks. Titmouse means small bird, coming from *mase*, the Anglo-Saxon word for bird, and *tit*, from the Icelandic word for small.

Tufted titmice remain in stable flocks during the winter, and groups of four to six birds feed together in open grassland over a twenty-acre range. The groups may be a mated pair and their offspring from the previous summer, but no one's sure if they're related or not. During the winter, the birds feed on seeds and often visit feeders. Titmice are insectivorous birds. They use their short, slender bills to pick small insects off leaves and twigs.

Close relatives of the chickadees, they also frequently visit feeders and use the familial acrobatic skills to feed from hanging suet feeders. In fact, several titmouse behaviors are similar to the chickadee's. They'll eat from other feeders as well, and enjoy baked goods, shelled peanuts and hearts, hulled or whole sunflower seeds, nutmeats, safflower, Niger, and hummingbird nectar. Titmice will eat at a swaying, swinging feeder, grabbing seeds and flying to safety to eat them. The titmouse rarely visits feeders singly, so there are often four or five others waiting to feed.

In the late winter, courtship begins and the small flocks break up. The males define and defend territories, and the younger members of the flock probably are forced out to find new ground while the older male remains around the wintering grounds. The males sing a short note, *peer, peer, peer*, to advertise their presence, and once a female shows interest, the male begins mate feeding, offering the female choice tidbits of food to woo her. As the female is fed, she gives a continuous call, *wheee wheee wheee*, and quivers her wings. The pair finds a tree cavity or nestbox for their family-to-be and builds a nest, lining it with soft material like fur or plant down. By the early summer, the fledglings begin traveling and feeding with their parents, the only clutch raised over the summer. The juveniles look like their parents except they lack the characteristic black patch on the forehead. The titmouse takes advantage of abandoned wood-pecker cavities for nesting.

BIRDMESS SCORE

Use this chart to determine for yourself whether this species is messy at *your* feeder. By scoring each bird you'll be able to better decide which birds to attract and which to deter.

Number of birds at one time:

Seed scattering :
(0=none 3=low 6=medium 9=high)

Poop producing :
(0=none 3=low 6=medium 9=high)

Other:
(feathers left behind; moving twigs around the yard;
0=none 3=low 6=medium 9=high)

Is this species accompanied by other species?
(0=no 6=yes)

TOTAL:

TOWHEE

Towhees are sparrows. The rufous-sided towhee covered here is the most common backyard visitor, but others include the Albert's, California, Canyon, and green-tailed. Towhees, named for their call, which they use to keep track of their mates in the dense brush where they live, stay close to cover. The rufous-sided towhee, a seven- to eight-inch bird, lives from southern Canada to Florida. You're likely to hear them before you see them as they move around noisily in the leaves in dense brush. If you do spot one, look for a bird with a brown (female) or black (male) back and head with rust sides and a white breast. In the yard and garden, they're likely in thickets, hedges, and brush piles. Towhees stay close to the ground, usually in brush or shrubs, and hunt for insects and seeds on the ground.

They pounce on the ground with both feet, scrape surface litter back, and look for exposed seeds and insects. In the warm spring and summer months, about half their diet comes from the insects they find. The rest of the year, they eat seeds and berries. In particular, they enjoy the fruits of the serviceberry, elderberry, and the blueberry. Towhees feed at ground feeders, tables, or shelves, and only visit feeders close to dense cover where they can hide easily. They eat millet, mixed seed, sunflower seed, nutmeats, Niger, suet mixtures, peanut meats and hearts, fruit, and cracked corn. Sometimes they come to hanging feeders if they're particularly hungry, but they persist in their scratching and spill seeds everywhere. Towhees nest deep in the thickets where they roost, hide, and feed, often building the nest on or near the ground if the cover isn't good enough higher up.

 **BIRDMESS SCORE**

Use this chart to determine for yourself whether this species is messy at *your* feeder. By scoring each bird you'll be able to better decide which birds to attract and which to deter.
Number of birds at one time:
Seed scattering :
(0=none 3=low 6=medium 9=high)
Poop producing :
(0=none 3=low 6=medium 9=high)
Other:
(feathers left behind; moving twigs around the yard;
0=none 3=low 6=medium 9=high)
Is this species accompanied by other species?
(0=no 6=yes)
TOTAL:

WOODPECKER

Including the flickers and sapsuckers, you can count twenty-two species of North American woodpeckers. Most common at the feeding stations: common flicker, yellow-bellied sapsucker, and the red-headed, downy, hairy, and red-bellied woodpecker. Woodpeckers use their thick bills to chisel into wood to find insects, sap, and grubs. Special adaptations for feeding include a strengthened skull and special cradling of the brain to withstand the shocks of hammering. The extra-long tongue is attached to a bone at its root and rests in a special groove above the right nostril until it's called into service. Then it can shoot two or three inches from the beak to pick up an escaping insect. The tip is covered with sticky mucus and often has fleshy barbs to help pick up insects. The sapsucker drills holes into the soft phloem layer under the bark to feed on oozing sap. An added plus: insects are attracted to the sap, and the bird eats them too.

Woodpeckers remain associated with their mates year-round, becoming a little more loosely attached during the winter. The pair continues to defend their territory year-round, so it is usual to have only the two birds visiting a feeding station unless it happens to be right on the edge of a territory, when several individuals may visit.

All woodpecker visitors like suet and suet mixtures. Others also eat meat scraps, nut and sunflower meats, cracked corn, chicken feed, baked goods, and raisins. The red-bellied has the most catholic tastes and will even forage on ground level. Get the woodpeckers started with suet and then add new offerings like suet mixtures, sunflower seed, peanut hearts, shelled or unshelled peanuts, nutmeats, American cheese, fruit, and hummingbird nectar. Since they feed singly and travel alone or in pairs, woodpeckers make pretty good visitors. To keep the suet accessible only to birds that can cling to the sides and bottom of a rigid suet feeder, cover the top with a dome to prevent starlings from perching there and pecking at the suet.

A woodpecker may discover food sources in the yard in addition to the suet and soon begin chipping away at trees infested with insect pests. Only the small downy woodpecker doesn't actually dig large holes in the tree, since it feeds on small insects just under the surface of the bark. Other woodpeckers go deeper and dig out wood chips as they excavate, making quiet, irregular knocking sounds as they dig. The rhythmic rat-a-tat-tat heard between early spring and midsummer is drumming done by a male or female to announce its presence to potential mates and to defend the territory. Drumming takes the place of singing and calling used by other birds in the mating season. A woodpecker chooses a resonant surface for drumming—aluminum siding, a hollow tree, or metal gutters—and usually does little damage. From time to time, buildings have insect infestations that attract a woodpecker, but then the drumming sound will be irregular and quieter than the attention-getting drumming.

Common Flicker

The common flicker comes in three varieties: the yellow-shafted, the gilded, and the red-shafted, all three formerly catalogued as separate species. The differences are only cosmetic. What the common flickers share is a brown back with black bars and spots, a crescent-shaped black spot on the breast, and a brown and gray head. The red markings vary from a red marking on the nape to a red whisker mark. Flickers are resident coast to coast across the U.S. with the exception of central Texas, where they only winter. They prefer open woods, grown-over pastures and logging areas, river groves, desert washes, and shade trees.

Flickers commonly eat ants, about half their diet, as well as other insects. They will feed on the ground, but usually they search for insects in trees. In the fall and winter, they become more dependent on other food sources and get half their diet from vegetable matter. They'll eat fruits and berries from the poison ivy, tupelo, hackberry, dogwood, wild cherry, grape, blueberry, holly, red cedar, and bayberry, as well as acorns, other nuts and seeds, and grass and weed seed. Flickers also eat seeds and fruit, especially avocado and orange crops in California. At the feeder, they especially enjoy suet, peanut butter, and bakery goods.

Flickers chisel out nesting cavities in trunks or stubs of dead trees because they're not as strong as other woodpeckers, who can excavate an opening in a live tree as well. They'll also excavate telephone poles, fence posts, buildings, and saguaro cactus, and will use special nesting boxes if the starlings don't beat them to it.

Yellow-bellied Sapsucker

The yellow-bellied sapsucker's colorful name aptly describes its appearance and diet. The eight- to nine-inch bird has a red crown and throat, a black mottled back and wings, and a yellow underside. At one time of the year or another, they come to most parts of the country. They winter in the southern U.S. and breed from the Rocky Mountains east to the mid-Atlantic and New England, skipping over the plains states. They prefer woodlands, aspen groves, river bottoms, and most wooded locations near openings. They tend to breed in aspen groves in Canada or western mountain ranges.

Sapsuckers rely on tree sap as a major food source. They drill rows of holes into the phloem layer of the tree, eating the cambium as well as the nutritious sap that oozes out. They return to the same sap wells to feed again and again, as do other birds and mammals when the sapsucker isn't around. Insects attracted to the sweet sap provide an easy meal for the sapsucker, who relies on insects and their eggs and larvae for a good portion of its diet. They also feed on the fruits of the dogwood, holly, Virginia creeper, red cedar, hackberry, elderberry, grape, sassafras, poison ivy, poison oak, and wild cherry. At the winter feeder, the sapsucker will take suet, peanut butter, bakery goods, jelly, and sugar water from a hummingbird feeder if it can perch.

Red-headed Woodpecker

The red-headed woodpecker is one of the few woodpeckers that lives up to its name. The eight- to nine-inch bird has a completely red head, neck, and upper breast. It prefers open, cut-over land and frequently lives in small towns and cities, along roads, and in open country. The redhead commonly lives in the eastern U.S. and often migrates west and north during the breeding season. Competition from starlings for nesting sites and a high mortality rate from

125

automobile run-ins combine to make the red-headed woodpecker rare in parts of its range.

Downy Woodpecker

The downy woodpecker is the smallest of the family, about six inches long, and not especially downy. Except for the size difference, the downy is tough to tell from the hairy woodpecker, a much larger but similar bird. Both have white backs and spotted wings, and the males have a red patch on the back of their heads. Both the downy and the hairy woodpecker have great individual variation, and if you keep close tabs, you'll learn to recognize different birds. The downy woodpecker frequents forests, woodlots, orchards, willows, and shade trees, which takes it from rural areas to suburban gardens to city parks. It ranges coast to coast across southern Canada and the U.S. with the exception of the arid southwest. The downy's small size helps when it wants to visit winter feeding stations, and it's perhaps the most common visitor among woodpeckers. The downy relies mostly on animal matter for food: insects, their larvae, and eggs it excavates from trees. It varies its diet with berries from poison ivy, dogwood, Virginia creeper, serviceberry, and tupelo; tree seeds, acorns, and nuts. At the feeder, it likes suet, peanut butter, nuts, bakery goods, and cracked corn. The downy excavates a cavity in a live or dead tree and lines the bottom with wood chips. It will also use nest boxes. Downies will nest in the same tree with the hairy woodpecker and generally tolerate its presence in the area, but they won't bear other downy woodpeckers.

Hairy Woodpecker

The hairy woodpecker, a large, nine-inch bird, appears to be an overgrown downy woodpecker, but look closely at the beak. It is large, more than half the depth of its head. They have the same white back and patterned wings and males have the same red head marking as the downy woodpecker. Hairy woodpeckers live in forests, woodlands, river groves, and shade trees, and share many behaviors with the downy woodpecker.

Red-bellied Woodpecker

The red-bellied woodpecker remains resident throughout its range from the Great Lakes area south to the Gulf states and east to the mid-Atlantic states. Its zebra-striped back, red cap, and white rump help identify it, but don't strain to find the red belly; it's white. The female only has a red nape, not a redhead. The red-bellied woodpecker lives in woodlands, groves, orchards, and towns, wherever there are big, old trees. It eats more vegetable matter than most woodpeckers and forages in low shrubs and on the ground for acorns and other nuts. It also eats fruits and berries from the grape, bayberry, dogwood, elderberry, palmetto, Virginia creeper, and poison ivy. At the feeder it enjoys suet, nuts, cracked corn, and sunflower seed. The red-bellied woodpecker will eat fruit set out in the spring. They chisel cavities into dead or diseased maples, pines, willows, and elms or just use an offered birdhouse for their nests.

 **BIRDMESS SCORE**

Use this chart to determine for yourself whether this species is messy at *your* feeder. By scoring each bird you'll be able to better decide which birds to attract and which to deter.

Number of birds at one time:

Seed scattering :
(0=none 3=low 6=medium 9=high)

Poop producing :
(0=none 3=low 6=medium 9=high)

Other:
(feathers left behind; moving twigs around the yard;
0=none 3=low 6=medium 9=high)

Is this species accompanied by other species?
(0=no 6=yes)

TOTAL:

WREN

There are nine types of wren, all alert, terribly cheerful little birds: Bewick's, cactus, canyon, Carolina, house, marsh, rock, sedge, and winter. They use their tails as signal flags, conveying agitation, aggression, or submission. All wrens have long, thin, slightly decurved bills and range in size from four to six inches long. Most are brown above and white or light brown below, only differentiated by slight differences in size and markings.

They're almost totally insectivorous, but may visit winter feeding stations for high-protein offerings. When they come, they look for American cheese, baked goods, hulled sunflower seeds, chopped nuts, peanut hearts, fresh fruit, suet and suet mixtures, nutmeats, and hummingbird nectar. Usually the Carolina, winter (eastern U.S.), and house (western U.S.) wrens visit feeders.

Carolina Wren
The five-inch, reddish brown Carolina wren sports conspicuous white eyebrow stripes, and if that's not enough to help you identify it, it's going to be the largest wren in its eastern range. Resident to the eastern U.S., they live in tangles, brushy undergrowth, suburban gardens, and towns, but even when they live around people, they're easy to miss because they're so timid and wary. In the far northern reaches of their range, many wrens die over a hard winter when they can't find enough food to keep warm and survive.

They forage on the ground for insects and their eggs and larvae. They manage to find animal matter for food most of the year; only ten percent of their diet come from plant sources. Try feeding them suet, peanut butter, peanut hearts, chopped nuts, sunflower seeds, and baked goods.

Carolina wrens, like some of the other wrens, are known for their unusual choices of nesting sites: old tin cans, abandoned furniture, and other unlikely cavities. Carolina wrens almost always nest in cavities, but they'll also build a nest in the fork of a tree if necessary. Any exposed nest is built with a roof and side entrance. The nest is a bulky assemblage of diverse natural material. The male and female build the nest together over a week or two. The female lays five to seven creamy-white eggs splotched with reddish brown. She incubates them for about two weeks before they hatch, and both parents have to get to hopping to bring enough insects to feed the hungry nestlings. After the young leave the nest for the first time, the male often takes over their care while the female gets busy building a new nest and laying another clutch of eggs. They won't have time to raise more than two broods, and the nesting season usually ends in July.

Winter Wren

The winter wren looks a lot like the house wren except it has a much stubbier tail, giving it a roly-poly appearance. Its barred breast and light line over the eye also help differentiate it from the house wren, with whom it shares some of its range. Winter wrens are resident through the Appalachian mountains and along the northern West Coast, but they breed in southern Canada and winter in the eastern U.S. They live in woodland underbrush in the winter and conifer forests in breeding season. They don't venture far from the dense undergrowth of the forests where they live, but occasionally they visit nearby yards. The resident winter wrens appreciate roosting boxes that will help them survive the cold nights when they can't find suitable dense brush for protection. The same overwintering wrens may appreciate a food handout and may eat suet, nuts, or baked goods. Males usually return from wintering rounds first and set about building decoy nests, often out in the open to attract mates. They nest close to the ground, often among the roots of a fallen tree, on river and stream banks, and even in abandoned buildings.

House Wren

This gray-brown bird has a light eye ring and no facial striping. It's resident along the West Coast, in New England, and in maritime Canada. It breeds throughout southern Canada and the U.S. except for the Gulf states, where it winters. It lives in open woods, thickets, towns, and gardens, and often nests in bird boxes. As the name implies, the house wren likes to live around people. Patios or yards surrounded by trees and shrubs attract the small, drab bird for feeding and nesting in the warm months and for food offerings in the cold ones.

The wrens rarely eat anything but insects, but in the hard times in early spring and late fall, they'll visit feeding stations to take suet, baked goods, or nutmeats.

Males return from migration first and build several nests to attract females to their territories. When they finally select a mate and a site, the females destroy the structure and build a new one more to their liking. The cavity nesters choose a wide variety of sites, anything from a tree cavity to an old shoe, and they control up to a half acre around the site. They're quick to use nest boxes built to suit them, and will use the hanging gourd types sold in so many stores. It's best to set out several so the male has plenty of sites to build in.

BIRDMESS SCORE

Use this chart to determine for yourself whether this species is messy at *your* feeder. By scoring each bird you'll be able to better decide which birds to attract and which to deter.

Number of birds at one time:

Seed scattering :

(0=none 3=low 6=medium 9=high)

Poop producing :

(0=none 3=low 6=medium 9=high)

Other:

(feathers left behind; moving twigs around the yard;

0=none 3=low 6=medium 9=high)

Is this species accompanied by other species?

(0=no 6=yes)

TOTAL:

3

Keeping Messy Birds and Other Creatures at Bay

FEEDERS THAT DISCOURAGE THE VULGAR ELEMENT

SOME FEEDERS ARE designed to attract ground-feeding birds. Some feeders are designed with squirrel prevention in mind. Some feeders are made for windows; others for vertical poles; others to be hung from trees or suspended from horizontal poles. Still other feeders are made to look good first, and be functional second.

Yet no feeder is designed from the perspective of keeping bird mess to a minimum. Most of the companies that manufacture feeders assume, like the general public, that birdfeeding is going to be messy and no birdfeeding hobbyist cares about bird mess. Still, despite the fact that feeders are not designed with neatness in mind, some feeders are tidier than others.

First are hummingbird feeders. Hummingbirds needs are simple: sweet water. Sugar water doesn't leave any shells and hummingbirds make hardly any poop. If you want to both feed birds and have a yard you can use—or a window you can look out of—there couldn't be a smarter idea than setting up hummingbird feeders in your yard. Hummingbirds are attracted to red, so while you're at it, hang out

135

some red socks, pants, handkerchiefs: you can attract hummingbirds and dry your laundry simultaneously.

As a general rule, the smaller the feeder, the better it is at keeping the mess at bay. Feeders that allow only one bird at a time to feed are best. Take-a-number feeders work well because many flocking birds such as finches don't like to wait their turn and will travel to your neighbor's yard if there's a line at your feeder. While it's not the purpose of this book to rate feeders, small window feeders, such as the Aspects Company's window feeders, and small pole-mounted feeders such as Bird-in-Hand, are good bets because they allow only a single bird at a time to feed (most of the time). On the following page is a short list of some single birdfeeders that can be filled with whole peanuts. (Remember to use peanuts. Filling a one-bird-at-a-time feeder with sunflower seeds still will produce shell and seed spillage. Combining a single birdfeeder with peanuts gives you a better anti-mess system.)

With the exception of hummingbird feeders, use pole-mounted feeders in your yard. (Window feeders are always fine.) Hanging feeders are more affected by the wind than are pole-mounted feeders: a swift wind can empty your feeder faster than a family of ravenous squirrels. And speaking of squirrels, pole-mounted feeders are easier to protect from those critters. Squirrels are infamous for their ability to knock the seed out of hanging feeders—and to knock down the entire hanging feeder, creating a mini–Exxon Valdez spill. It's also easier to put a seed catcher that works beneath a pole-mounted feeder. Seed catchers, trays or upside-down baffles, actually serve two functions. They keep spilled seed from polluting the ground below and they catch bird poop before it has a chance to make your green lawn look like bottles of White Out™ were poured all over. If you employ a seed catcher, remove the seed often from the catcher.

SINGLE-BIRD FEEDERS (WHEN FILLED WITH WHOLE PEANUTS)

Select-A-Bird	Bird-in-Hand
Artline Window Birdfeeder	Carruth Studio Kitty Feeder

FEEDERS THAT MAKE A MESS, BUT CAN BE MADE LESS MESSY

If you already own one of these feeders, or have your heart set on one, don't despair; read on about how you can adapt your feeder to make it less messy.

Cardinal Barn	Family Feeder
Hanging suet baskets	
without hoods or baffles	The SSP, Steel Squirrel-Proof Feeder
The Fiesta	Nelson Products Foiler

Another way of reducing the amount of mess your birds create is to use bowl feeders on poles. These naturally trap hulls, so there's no direct spillage. The smaller the better. If you use a large bowl feeder, don't fill it all the way; this will keep the hulls from scattering as the birds plow through for more seeds. Most bowl feeders are meant to be hung, so you will have to use your ingenuity to adapt them to pole mounting. The Droll Yankee X-1 Seed Saver lets you adjust the height of the top baffle and bottom bowl to restrict the kinds of birds that dine. A few other feeders also allow you to adjust the space between the two bowls. By the way, be sure to keep the seed dry by covering the feeder with a large baffle or by putting small holes in the bowl to drain rainwater. Seed that gets wet can become moldy, especially during the warmer weather, and mold can make birds sick. With bowl feeders it's especially important to clean them regularly. Remember, don't touch a feeder with bare hands, and wash with hot soapy water if you do.

Look for feeders with a single perch and a single, small hole. This ensures that only one bird at a time can eat.

What else makes for a less messy feeder? As I mentioned, small is beautiful when it comes to feeders. Not only are smaller feeders likely to have just one feeding port, but because they are small they are less visible to many birds. Wild birds that feast at feeders tend to be attracted to feeders that display large amounts of seed. Small feeders are more discreet, and probably will attract only the smarter birds, or the birds with better eyesight, or something like that.

Window feeders are usually less messy than feeders mounted on poles. There's only one side that birds can approach on most window feeders, as compared to many pole-mounted feeders, which birds can approach from 360 degrees. These feeders are less conspicuous and won't be spotted by most birds. Some messy birds don't like to eat at window feeders (but alas, finches do), but all neat birds like window feeders. Crows abhor window feeders.

Would but could we transmute messy birds into neat birds, the world would be perfect. Unfortunately, untidiness is a matter of genetics and there's nothing you can do to turn a messy bird into one who's a member of the clean-plate club. Fortunately, you can con semi-neat birds into behaving neatly by adapting feeders so that these birds cannot appear in groups.

POSITIONING AND MODIFYING YOUR FEEDER TO MAKE IT LESS MESSY

Why throw away a (nearly) perfectly good feeder, just because it makes your yard look like a landfill? Many feeders can be adapted to keep the mess away (some, such as the metal spring-weighted feeders, can't.) The first thing to do is block all feeding ports except for one. If you are using a vertical feeder, keep the bottom hole open and obstruct the others. The objective is to allow only one bird at a time to eat. You'll avoid the bird equivalent of a high school cafeteria food fight.

Once some neat birds have discovered your feeder, paint or cover the feeder so that no other birds will spot it. Wallpaper and designer contact paper will work as well as paint—just as long as the feeder is completely opaque save for the feeding port. (You'll have to check the feeder regularly to see if it's empty.) Birds locate food by sight,

not smell, so if uninvited birds can't see the food, they won't raid your feeder. The fewer birds, the less the mess. There's something pleasing about having the same birds appear at your feeder—you almost get to know their personalities, their predilections. When these neat birds who know your feeder pass away or find more interesting feeders, you can temporarily put up a second, uncovered feeder, or uncover this one to attract a new crop of neat birds.

Convert your hanging feeder into a pole-mounted feeder. Nearly all hanging feeders can be made to rest on a pole. As I mentioned earlier, pole feeders spill less seed than hanging feeders that sway in the breeze or move when squirrels jump on them. The difference is enormous. The only requirement is that the feeder have a flat bottom. If the feeder already has a pole-mounting structure, so much the better. If it doesn't, solder the feeder to a pole with any lead solder. The heat alone should melt the plastic and make it adhere to the pole. Alternatively, mount a platform feeder on top of the pole and put your hanging feeder on top of that. Use the platform feeder as a base and seed catcher, not as a feeder itself. And don't forget the appropriate anti-squirrel baffles.

Protect your feeder from starlings, the worst offenders in the bird mess department. One attribute of starlings makes them easy to thwart: starlings cannot eat upside down; that is, from below. They don't like to fly up into things. That's why you won't see starlings at a GSP feeder. Put a hood above the feeding portal on your feeder and you'll reduce the chance that starlings will visit you. Similarly, cover the top and sides of a suet basket, leaving only the bottom exposed.

There's a sneaky way to turn your finch feeder into a feeder that attracts only goldfinches. Cut the perch down from 1 inch to ½ inch. Purple and house finches can't alight on short perches, while goldfinches can. The frustrated purple and house finches will go elsewhere.

NEAT NON-FEEDER STRATEGIES

YOU CAN ATTRACT wild birds without having feeders in your yard. Get rid of those feeders and enjoy messless birds! Before birdfeeders, birds got by on wild seed, nuts, fruits, and insects. If you plant your backyard with attractive flowers, shrubs, bushes, and trees, birds will come to visit, but in smaller numbers because the food source is less concentrated than it is at a feeding station. By approaching the hobby this way, you avoid one of the two problems, massive seed/hull spillage. (There will still be bird droppings, but far less than if you had feeders.) Feederless birdfeeding is also less expensive than birdfeeding (there's no seed to buy), and requires less maintenance (birdfeeders should be cleaned regularly with hot, soapy water).

Most birders never approach the hobby this way because, well, after all it's called *birdfeeding*. A more sensible way to look at the hobby is to call it *attracting wild birds*. That's your objective, anyway. Making the conceptual leap from birdfeeding to attracting wild birds shouldn't be difficult, because the result is the same: a yard wild with birds.

If you want birds, just look at your yard the way a bird would and add any missing ingredients. Birds don't live by bread crumbs alone. When they survey a landscape, they're looking for three things. Does the area provide food, water, or cover—a place to nest, roost, and rest? They must have all three in reasonable proximity to one another, but not necessarily in the same yard, so grow sunflowers while you wait for the oak to get big enough to support nests. Provide water while you're waiting for the flowers to seed. It's likely that birds will find sources for their other needs in nearby yards, fields, and woods.

Feeding and sheltering birds with plants and trees has advantages over feeding stations. For one, you won't have to fill and refill feeders daily, and for another, bird visitors won't be concentrated around a feeding source where they'll leave droppings and scatter seeds.

Instead of birdfeeders, consider planting sources of food and cover in your backyard. Every part of the country offers a suitable environment for plants and flowers that wild birds like to eat. Compared to feeders, plants and flowers have many advantages. First, most plants look better than feeders. The average feeder fits somewhere between homely and unsightly; they remind me of garages: practical, but not constructed with esthetics foremost. Lawns were never designed with Lucite™and metal in mind. Plants and flowers, on the other hand, simply go better with lawns. There's nothing like a lush yard, except for a lush yard that's plentiful with wild birds. Manicured lawns discourage birds.

This is a good place to add that you can even put bird-attracting plants and flowers on your windowsill. There's no great rule book of birdfeeding that says birds are only attracted to manmade feeders. Believe me, birds love to hang out at plants and flowers. Plants on your windowsill will make it almost completely mess-free. A plant or two or three is the perfect solution for the apartment dweller whose building prohibits any kind of feeder and strictly enforces this regulation with local, self-appointed anti-feeder police. Many plants and flowers that can be grown in a backyard can also be put in pots. Geraniums come immediately to mind, as do roses and hollies. So if you are an apartment dweller, read the rest of this chapter with ebullient anticipation.

What plants? The quick answer is: many plants. If humming-birds are your desire, any red flowering plants will do. A potpourri of roses that bloom throughout the warm weather months will work wonders. Plant a variety of flowers. Plants, flowers, and vines that attract hummingbirds include foxgloves, red geraniums, petunias, spider flowers, lilies, mimosa trees, coral bells, azaleas, day lilies, fuchsias, beauty bushes, and trumpet honeysuckles.

Landscaping for the birds is a little different from gardening for yourself. Perhaps you'd choose carrots, tomatoes, roses, or colum-bine for your property, but your basic backyard bird won't choose your yard over your neighbor's because you have great carrots. Try to make your yard into a replica of the natural environment, which is not the same thing as letting weeds grow waist-high up to your door. Landscaping to attract birds doesn't have to mean unkempt, overgrown yards or a finely-manicured English garden. Effort re-quired ranges from a few plants in a patio container to a landscaped pond; each strategy brings some backyard bird visitors.

By the way, unkempt lawns do better at attracting birds, so if you want to use this as an official excuse not to mow, you can quote me. Lawns that exceed the unofficial U.S. Government Accepted Level of Grass Blade Height for Suburban America of 1.45 inches don't necessarily look unsightly (after all, this book's purpose is to eliminate mess, not create more chaos) especially when surrounded by lush, flowering plants. Frankly, I have a personal preference for lawns that are a little overgrown, that have a dandelion or two or twenty growing in them, that aren't the subject and object of 100-decibel lawn mowing. A tourist-brochure perfect lawn in my mind—and in reality—means a lawn thickly covered with pesticide and herbicide. Not the kind of lawn you'd want your kids playing on. The amount of time and energy that goes into maintaining a pristine lawn could be better spent enjoying it. You know: watching the birds, resting and reading a book, playing with a Frisbee; that sort of thing. Nature isn't orderly, and it is unnatural to try and make it so.

Few birds actually live year-round deep in the forest, where it's difficult to see as well as to maneuver around all the trees and shrubs. Most birds live around edges or margins, in the places where open fields or wetlands meet forest. These productive edges provide easy access to a variety of plant foods as well as to insects that thrive in open fields and wetlands. The understory, or low trees and bushes in a forest, shelters birds from danger and inclement weather, while the high trees provide a handy lookout. Edges may appear abruptly, as when a cleared field abuts a forested area, or the forest growth may gradually disappear as you move outward, dense trees and understory blending into small trees and brush and then giving way to a few bushes and grassland. Edges also occur in open land when an oasis of trees or bushes appears, often around a water source.

Birds generally choose a variety of habitats in their ranges, moving from open-country oases to forest openings, depending on the food resources available. A small grove of trees within a large field may attract bluebirds looking for a handy hunting perch, or they may hunt from the edge overlooking open country, but they certainly wouldn't hunt in deep forest, where kinglets, thrushes, and vireos make their home. In addition, birds exploit different levels of a habitat. Hunting birds like martins or mockingbirds generally like the upper reaches of the trees, where they can see around them, while shyer, more nervous birds stay in the dense undergrowth where they're safe from danger.

Today, as more land comes under development, birds are looking for likely backyard homes for themselves. Although some clearing of the heavily forested eastern U.S. was good for bird populations because it increased feeding grounds, additional clearing destroys precious nesting territories as well as food and water sources. Since backyards often approximate an edge or margin, birds look to our territory with an eye to control some of it for themselves. Backyards become transitional zones for birds, a welcome change from the surrounding habitat.

It's easy enough to make your property resemble the natural oases or edges birds like. Basically, birds want what they don't have. In forested areas, they're looking for a nice, protected clearing where they can hunt bugs and forage for seeds, but in a clearing, they'd like to have a few shrubs or trees for hunting, protection, and food. In the western U.S. where trees are scarce, backyard trees become especially important to the birds in search of a perch. City homes with yards provide greenways for birds, areas of haven and food in a desert of concrete. Big-city apartment dwellers have fewer choices in landscaping for the birds. Windowboxes of flowers won't attract the colorful nectar-feeding species; unfortunately, not all the trumpet flowers in the world will manage to bring hummingbirds to a Manhattan balcony. Still, house sparrows might come to a potted boxwood or other balcony-sized shrub or seed-bearing flower.

Some birds adapt especially well to new circumstances in civilization. Many trees—sycamores, ashes, elms, maples, and tupelos—that grow along streams in wet, compact soil also thrive along suburban streets—and so do the birds that live in them. Orioles, which before development nested in the very tips of branches overhanging water, today choose to build in suburban trees overhanging the street. The roadway inhibits access to the nest from the ground in the same way that water does, and the fragile branches won't support most predators.

Still, birds won't adjust to circumstances entirely foreign to their natural habitat. Falcons that adapt to city skyscrapers originally hunted and lived among high trees and canyons. Without telephone poles, high buildings, trees, and other high perches, the falcons wouldn't be able to hunt.

Birds survey all the resources in the area, not just the bird-lover's half acre of fenced property, so whether the neighborhood abuts a wildlife refuge or a golf course or a sanitary landfill influences the birds that come to visit. If there aren't any trees for miles around, don't be disappointed if you don't get woodpeckers; learn what birds are attracted to the surrounding habitat and landscape with plants they like.

Landscaping for the birds is more than just planting a few trees and flowers. Remember, you're creating an edge effect, large or small, tall or short. You need to provide depth and texture in the landscape. Pay attention to the layers of the backyard. Is there a goodly portion of shrubs and small trees for smaller, shy birds? Are seed-bearing flowers accessible to the brushy cover? Is there an equal proportion of deciduous to evergreen trees? Some birds prefer one kind over another for nesting. Trim and prune your bushes? Heavens, no! Don't bother: the thicker the bush, the more birds.

If you have the space, work on a large scale. Create an edge of tall trees with a thick understory around the perimeter of your yard, and then put in flowerbeds in the open areas. Plant an oasis of small trees and shrubs around a birdbath or pond. If you have a small yard, use the space well. Plant shrubs along sidewalks, drives, patios, the open areas that are dangerous to birds, so they'll have places to roost, hide, and even feed.

A variety of plants, flowers, trees, shrubs, and grasses will attract plenty of birds. Vary the species of foliage you incorporate into your landscaping.

THE BEST PLANTS FOR ATTRACTING
A VARIETY OF MESSLESS BIRDS

Trees

Alder	Beech
Birch	Buckthorn
Crabapple	Dogwood
Elm	Greenbrier
Hackberry	Holly
Juniper	Maple
Mulberry	Oak
Pine	Plum cherry
Red cedar juniper	Sour gum
Sweet gum	Sycamore
Tupelo	

Shrubs and Vines

Bayberry	Elderberry
Honeysuckle	Raspberry
Sumac	Virginia creeper

Plants

Geranium	Pokeberry
Strawberry	Sunflower

FOOD

Bird food is as variable as birds themselves. While finches prefer seeds, woodpeckers hunt insects and hummingbirds seek nectar, and each food requires different plantings and maintenance. For instance, planting a tree is a back-taxing experience. First you have to dig a huge pit, mix a little organic matter and sand around the bottom and sides, and then backfill the excavated dirt over the new tree's rootball. And then you have to water, water, water. Annual gardens need digging and planting every year. So you see, the effort varies.

Some landscaping for the birds is merely putting off what some might consider routine maintenance. Most people immediately identify sunflowers as a good bird food source, but they're a little slower to consider the food production possibilities of a diseased tree branch that will support the insects so attractive to woodpeckers and nuthatches. Unless a tree is in danger of falling because of root rot, consider leaving diseased and dying trees on your property. Trim limbs back to three- or four-inch stubs if they're in danger of falling and causing damage. The trees attract insects, and the dead wood makes it easier for cavity nesters to chisel out a home. No one likes to see a tree die, but bird visitors will help make up for the lost beauty of a healthy tree. Chickadees, nuthatches, and woodpeckers will visit to extract insects from the bark and wood.

Birds like many of the same trees we do: cherry, dogwood, holly, alder, ash, birch, elm, beech, hawthorn, maple, mulberry (we like them as long as they're not over the porch or entryway), oak, pine, poplar, sassafras, sweet gum, sycamore, tupelo, and walnut. Birds appreciate the flowers and exotic plants, too; look for plants that bloom and bear fruit profusely so there's always plenty of food available to the birds. In addition seek plants that fruit in spring, summer, and fall so the birds have food available during the slim months.

Spring is an especially hard time for birds. The cool months provide few fruits, insects, or seeds, and birds are hard pressed to prepare for the strenuous season of mating and nesting to come. Plants that hold seeds and fruit over the winter and early-maturing fruits are especially important in the spring. Try holly, mountain ash, and sumac. Birds like bluebirds and mockingbirds eat fruit that remains on the tree over the winter if it doesn't become encrusted with ice. Late-fruiting trees and shrubs can provide food for birds that wouldn't normally visit a feeding station and will bring new birds into the yard.

Berry-producing plants are essential for anyone who longs for birdfeeding without mess. Berries are abundant during the summer, so cultivate plants that bear berries in the winter and spring. (A common misconception among bird feeders is that food is scarcest in winter. Actually, it's early springtime, before the new growth has emerged, when famine may strike birds.)

Most people think of seed when they think of bird food, and with good reason. Most birds eat seeds at one time or another during the year. In addition, insects are mighty scarce during the cold months, and birds in the colder states depend on seeds and nuts to get them through the season. A busy gardener can try pinks, sunflowers, zinnia, and other annuals to attract birds to the garden, while the trouble-free gardener may want to try perennials like the black-eyed Susan, goldenrod (get a package of meadow in a can), or statice. Sunflowers will probably reseed themselves with all the spillage from the feeding birds, so they're not too much trouble. Leave the dead flowers on the stalks over winter so the birds can feed on the seeds in the cold months. Trim shrubs and bushes back in the spring after the birds have harvested the seeds and fruit and sheltered there all winter.

Plant a shrubby understory around tall, shady trees to attract more birds—hummers especially like this.

Don't forget to leave some soil exposed beneath the shady understory. Birds will forage there for insects. Keep in mind that the scrubbier your yard, the more worms and ground crawling insects you'll have—that means more birds. Insects and worms bring in species that birdseed never attracts. You'll attract more hummingbirds with foliage than with feeders. And don't forget the fact that ruby-throated hummingbirds, the most common in North America, like to nest in birch, hemlock, maple, oak, and apple trees. Certainly the old standby, sunflower, works wonders in any yard. Plant as many as you like. They grow quickly. A bird alighting on a sunflower plant looks prettier than one sitting on a poop-covered feeder.

WATER

As I mentioned earlier, water actually attracts more birds than food. This is especially true in wintertime when free-flowing sources of water are scarce. Birdbaths won't eliminate the bird poop problem (though they will lessen it), but you won't, of course, have any seeds or hulls scattered about. If droppings aren't that big a concern to you, but seed debris is, then a birdbath is the way to go.

Birdbaths come in all varieties. A couple of points to keep in mind. First, the depth shouldn't be greater than two inches and the slope into the water should be gradual—this helps birds escape in the event of predators. Choose a bath that's not only easy to clean, but one that you are likely to clean. For many people, the more attractive the birdbath the greater the chance that they will keep it sanitary. This means a weekly wash (not such a chore because the water used to clean the bath is already on site.) *Please,* do clean the birdbath regularly: a messy birdbath is unsanitary for the birds and for you. If you plan to use your birdbath in winter, heat it. Birds can't peck through the ice to get at the water.

Unfortunately, you can't select particular species at a birdbath. But you will reduce the amount of mess made in your yard nonetheless. Indeed, you can dispense with seed entirely, and just deploy birdbaths. If you live in an apartment you can also have a birdbath.

Any of the rectangular suction-cup feeders such as the Duncraft Classic II or the generic feeders you find at hardware stores can be filled with water; so can round window feeders like the classic Droll Yankee Winner. Make sure these feeders don't have drainage holes if you're using them as baths. (Make sure they do have drainage holes if you are using them as feeders.) If the feeder has any holes, plug them with putty. Avoid glues because many glues react chemically with plastic, melting it. Avoid lead solder as well, because lead is toxic to birds and other critters. An advantage to offering birds water as opposed to food at your window is that because you aren't technically feeding birds you aren't violating your building's regulations against "birdfeeding." So there you have it, the secret to resolving your birdfeeding dilemma: don't feed the birds—give them a drink! Inspired apartment owners should also plant flowers and plants that are likely to attract birds. Nobody can complain about that, either. And while I'm talking about getting around apartment rules forbidding birdfeeding, let me suggest (quietly) putting some peanuts on your windowsill. Nobody from below or above is going to spot the nuts. Once you've attracted some birds, replace the peanuts with both hulled sunflower seeds and peanut butter—messless and invisible. Just don't tell anybody why it's your window that all the blue jays and chickadees are flocking to.

For homeowners, birds like running water even more than birdbaths. Drip devices, such as The Dripper, which attach to an outside garden hose faucet are guaranteed to bring birds to your yard. In just the right numbers, too, as a drip can't accommodate more than a couple of birds at the same time.

Almost any kind of outdoor fountain will work—not just those designed for birds. Keep in mind that whatever source of water you provide will become coated with occasional bird droppings and feathers, but that minor mess is more than made up for by the attractive birds. Most outdoor water fountains use continually circulating water, so that you don't have the equivalent of a leaking faucet. It's okay to add a tiny amount of chlorine—the kind you get for swimming pools—to the fountain. This will help prevent the growth of bacteria. How much chlorine? That answer involves a little math. Use the dilution proportions on the chlorine box to calculate how much chlorine your fountain requires, based on the ratio of the volume of water a pool holds to the volume of water your fountain holds. You will discover that a very, very small quantity of chlorine will do.

Water needs vary from bird to bird, but water sources are sure to attract bird visitors. If you choose to provide water, incorporate the birdbath or small pond into your landscaping scheme with plantings of small trees and shrubs nearby.

You can choose not to maintain ponds or feeders and water the birds when you water the yard. Lots of birds enjoy the misty spray of sprinklers in the morning and will run in and out of the falling droplets like little children.

NESTING, ROOSTING, AND LOITERING

Just like human parents who suddenly become aware of schools and services when they have a baby, birds become a mite more choosy about their surroundings when it comes to the serious business of nesting. The landscape determines what birds will stay in your yard through the nesting season. Some birds, like the northern oriole, migrate to North America for the nesting season, while others remain resident throughout the year or head for the far north.

Some birds only nest in deep deciduous or evergreen forests, so don't be hurt when they leave for more secluded parts. For those that remain, provide all sorts of choices: high shade trees with plenty of cover, low trees, dense brush, and dead trees; trees among other trees, trees with branches overhanging open space, trees and bushes close to a pond. Many birds choose impenetrable, thorny thickets for nesting; they like the multiflora rose or scarlet firethorn, for instance.

In the same vein, birdhouses in general give you all the pleasures of birdfeeding with none of the mess. Don't be shy—erect a house near your window so you can see the birds coming and going.

Different birds prefer different shapes and sizes of houses, as well as distinct entrance-hole sizes and hole heights (as measured from the base of the birdhouse.) You can determine which birds you attract by the kind of house you erect. In fact, birds are even more picky about the kind of house they roost in than they are about the kind of food they eat. By the way, there's nothing wrong with putting up several different species-specific houses if you want a variety of birds living in your yard.

If you have sufficient open space, erect a purple martin house. These birds have magnificent flight patterns and eat gobs of mosquitoes, too. There are plenty of purple martin houses on the market; I recommend picking one that's easy to clean, because you, not the martins, will have to do the annual cleaning before they take up residence each spring. Purple martins are most likely to nest colonially in the Eastern states.

CHARACTERISTICS OF BIRDHOUSES

Bird	Box Height (in)	Box Floor (in)	Entrance Height (in)	Entrance Diameter (in)	Height Above Ground (ft)
Bluebird	8–12	5x5	6–10	1½	4–6
Chickadee	8–10	4x4	6–8	1⅛	5–15
Titmouse	8–10	4x4	6–8	1¼	6–15
Nuthatch	8–10	4x4	6–8	1⅜	5–15
Downy Woodpecker	8–10	4x4	6–8	1¼	5–15
Purple Martin	10–11	6x6	6	2½	10–20
Pileated Woodpecker	16–24	8x8	12–20	3–4	15–25
Carolina Wren	6–8	4x4	4–6 (approx.)	5–12	1¼

Most bird boxes should be erected by the end of March, before mating season begins.

As an adjunct to erecting a birdhouse, put some nesting material in your yard. You can buy commercial nesting material, or cut some thread, yarn, string, and cotton and place it in a branch. Just about any material from your collection of sewing scraps will do. Birds will pick up the material in their beaks and carry it away to a nearby tree. Watching birds try to grab nesting material and carry it away is even more fun than watching them go after seed. It's really a treat to watch a tiny chickadee fly across your yard with a large piece of yarn in its beak.

Starlings and house sparrows are particularly adept at setting up housekeeping in the birdhouses intended for native species before the natives can manage to move in. These aggressive immigrants drive out many smaller, shyer birds, destroy nests and eggs, and generally make things rough for wrens, purple martins, bluebirds, and other desirable backyard birds. The only way to fight starling and sparrow intrusion is to daily destroy their attempts at nestmaking. Clear out all of their accumulated material and throw it away—maybe they'll take the hint.

In addition, throughout the year, birds need a place to hang out—low bushes for hiding, high tree branches for sighting prey, foliage-covered branches for nesting, or dense brush for roosting. On wicked cold winter nights, several small birds may squeeze into a birdhouse together to keep warm, so don't take the houses in for the winter. In addition to great chow, birds seek a quick getaway, and if feeding stations don't provide accessible cover, the birds won't want to visit. In the winter and during bad weather, birds like to find a little shelter. They'll often roost in bushes and trees that offer some protection from the elements. A roosting spot out of the wind often means the difference between death and survival on a cold winter night.

TOO MUCH OF A GOOD THING

You may reserve part of your yard for growing your own food, only to discover that the birds don't really understand concepts like "yours" and "mine." Before you know it, they're helping themselves

to corn, cherries, and helpless little seedlings. Birds and people eat many of the same fruits, and the birds even eat the flowers of fruit trees, so protecting these crops is a special challenge. You can try providing attractive food sources far from the target crop to lure the birds away, but the solution is iffy at best.

On a small scale, exclusion works best. Keep the birds away from the target crop from bloom through harvest with bird netting. Garden supply stores sell nets large enough to cover a fruit tree and long enough to cover row crops like strawberries. When you're protecting row crops, you'll need to first build a frame to support the netting, but you can just drape the net over the fruit tree. You can lay fine netting or mesh directly on the ground to discourage small-seed eaters like sparrows, and simply remove the barrier after the seeds have sprouted and the danger is past. Ultralight garden blankets that allow moisture and light to pass through will also help protect target seeds, sprouts, and fruits on the ground.

Besides exclusion, you have the option of trying to frighten the birds out of the garden. Scarecrows, rubber snakes, plastic owls, and aluminum pie plates tied to poles with string have limited effect; eventually the birds realize the strange objects are harmless and move in anyway. More effective solutions use random noise to scare the birds away. Exploding devices and guns work just fine as long as the neighbors don't object. Try criss-crossing monofilament line at various angles over the garden to prevent birds from landing in the patch and feasting. The strings confuse them, and they won't fly through them to get at the crops. Of course, they eventually figure out they can just walk under the string and eat all they want, but it's effective for a while, maybe long enough to get the crop in.

Of course, plenty of people figure the birds do more good than harm and let them eat what they want in return for insect eradication services. Nature designed bugs with birds in mind. Just when the birds need extra protein to feed hungry, growing nestlings, insects, grubs, and eggs become abundant. Most seed-eating birds turn to insects in the summer months. It doesn't take a rocket scientist to realize that fertilizers and pesticides you employ in the garden eventually build up in the birds' bodies, sometimes with deadly effect.

Someone once said, "Birds of a feather flock together." So what do you do about that? Just as some people trap and move squirrels away, you might consider exporting troublesome birds. This is a temporary solution, to be sure, but then again everything about life is temporary. Sparrows, pigeons, finches, and starlings are generally stupid enough to fall for the trap trick, and if you can reduce the messy bird population in your yard by a dozen or two, then you've gone a long way toward achieving your objective. Check with local and state regulations before you trap the birds, though. Laws protect most native songbirds, although there's little protection for the starlings, pigeons, and house sparrows. Traps, which cost about sixty dollars, can catch up to twenty sparrow-sized birds at one time, and are easy to use. They're fun, too. Look for traps that are designed so you don't have to handle the birds. Be sure to check the trap frequently, and move the birds as soon as the trap fills. In addition, move the birds at least a couple miles away so they visit somebody else's yard.

A FEW WORDS ABOUT SQUIRRELS AND OTHER ANIMALS THAT INVADE YOUR FEEDER

THE MOMENT YOU put out birdseed is the moment you discover that there are plenty of other critters that inhabit your yard. And if they don't inhabit your yard, they'll sure to pay a visit when your birdfeeder is out.

Let's face facts. Birds aren't the only hungry ones in the neighborhood. Squirrels, raccoons, opossums, skunks, snakes, cats, and other critters are likely to want to hang out where your birdfeeder is. Who wants what?

- Squirrels are going to try and try and try *and try* to get at your birdseed and they won't care a single bit about any mess they create along the way.

- Raccoons are interested in what you store in your cans outdoors. Never mind that they don't eat sunflower seed, they'll open every closed object, including metal birdfeeders.
- Deer will munch on any plants and flowers you're growing for the birds' benefit.
- Cats will go after the birds.
- Your neighbor's dog will fertilize your yard, making the birds' mess look positively antiseptic.
- Predatory birds such as hawks will pick off a songbird or two.
- Skunks are going to prowl around and woe be to the person who gets in the way.

So what to do about all these critters? Obviously, this subject deserves an entire book in itself. But there are some general principles you can use to combat these pesky and messy critters.

Unfortunately, the best advice I have to offer contradicts much of what I said earlier. Here it is: keep your yard as neat and as kempt as possible.

I know: I've told you that the taller your grass, the more plants you have, and the thicker the bushes, the better you'll do at attracting wild birds. So now why should you give your yard a crew cut? How to reconcile these two disparate propositions?

As a bird feeder you already know, whether consciously or subconsciously, that nature is chaotic. It is inherently messy, unpredictable, disorderly, and downright amusing. In other words, you will never have a perfect yard. There will always be some combination of birds, bird mess, trimmed lawn, unkempt lawn, other animals, and, alas, your neighbor's dogs.

But there are some clear steps you can take to try to achieve that elusive goal. First, keeping dog and cat food outside is a bad idea. What's yummy to a dog is also yummy to a raccoon or worse, a skunk. Here's food for thought: it's more expensive to keep dog food outdoors when other animals eat it.

Plant your shrubs, trees, flowers, and other bird-attracting foliage around the perimeter of your yard. This way, you'll encourage birds, but you will discourage critters from waltzing right through the middle of your property. The closer animals get to your house, the more they're interested in getting *inside* your house. Putting foliage on the perimeter of your property won't guarantee that this is where the critters will stay, but it won't provide incentive for them to run amok.

Walk around your house and take a look at it from an animal's perspective. Are there any openings that provide good nesting or entry sites? As the cold seasons approach, critters are going to view your house as a comfortable place to rest.

How is your seed stored? What's convenient for you may be convenient for animals, too. For example, leaving a plastic bag filled with sunflower seed or peanuts under your deck is asking for a visit from every squirrel in the vicinity. So then what? You could try putting the seed in a metal garbage can with a lid. Predictably, raccoons are going to pop open the can at night. And while raccoons aren't necessarily thrilled by sunflower seed, they will make a mess of the seed looking for stuff they do like to eat. Or are they making a mess to give you this message? Next time put out food *we* like.

You can try securing the garbage can with string, cord, bungie cord; but anything *not* made of metal, such as chains, will be chomped through by raccoons.

A FINAL MESSAGE

THERE ARE PLENTY of rules of thumb offered in this book. Feel free to ignore as many as you want. These are only guidelines for making your birdfeeding less messy, a worthwhile objective because it enhances the pleasure of attracting wild birds. I've tried to be creative where it helps, as in adapting window feeders to window baths. Experimentation is the key to birdfeeding. The advice in *Impeccable Birdfeeding* will certainly make your hobby neater and safer, but you will have to adapt these techniques to your particular house and lifestyle. Above all, have fun attracting wild birds.

While reading this book you may have had this thought: does emphasizing neat birdfeeding lessen the ability of birds to enjoy my feeder? Well, the honest answer to that is, maybe. After all, giving birds *everything* they want would make them happier. If you feel that the wild birds have been deprived, let me suggest the following ways to show your affection:

WHAT YOU CAN DO TO MAKE THE BIRDS VERY HAPPY

1. Buy a Doberman—it will keep all the cats in your neighborhood away!

2. Build a "gingerbread" house out of suet and put it in your yard.

3. Hire a plane to drop hulled sunflower seed over your neighborhood.

4. Leave copies of *Bird Fancy* magazine around for them to browse through.

5. Plant cotton so that birds will have ample nesting material.

6. Take a course in wild bird first aid.

7. Play tapes of wild birdsong, especially those of parrots and other exotic species, to give your wild birds a feeling that they're in a faraway place.

8. Get a birdcage and put a stuffed cat inside.

9. Grow peanuts.

10. Get legislation passed banning flying of radio-controlled airplanes that can hit birds.

11. Hire a $200-an-hour architect to build birdhouses in your yard.

12. Have tiny forks, knives, plates, and napkins made. Maybe the birds will learn to use these culinary implements.

13. Remove all glass doors that birds could fly into.

14. Encourage people to buy squirrel coats, thereby reducing the population of squirrels in your yard and increasing the amount of seed available for your birds.

15. When you go away, put birdseed in those automatic pet feeders.

16. Build a moat around your entire yard, filled with water. It won't keep the squirrels out, but the moat will keep the cats away.

17. Go to a gourmet store and buy gourmet nuts. Try pistachio. They're as expensive as ever, but if the birds like these nuts, let them enjoy!

18. Import worms for robins.

19. Get up early in the morning and do birdcalls.

20. Get a feeder shaped like a hand. Eventually birds will learn to alight on your own hand.

21. Paint a giant bull's-eye in the middle of your yard so that birds can spot it from hundreds of feet up.

22. If you don't have power or telephone lines running across your property, put some up. Birds like to perch on wires.

23. Leave your windows open all winter in case birds want to come inside to warm up.

24. Post no-squirrel signs. (The signs won't work, of course, but they will be a sign that you care.)

BIBLIOGRAPHY

America's Favorite Backyard Birds, Kit and George Harrison, Simon and Schuster, 1983

The Audubon Society Field Guide to North American Birds, Knopf, 1977

Backyard Bird Habitat, Jane and Will Curtis, Countryman Press, 1988

Feed the Birds, Helen Witty and Dick Witty, Workman Publishing Company, 1991

How to Attract Birds, Ortho Books, 1983

Peterson Field Guide Series, *Eastern Birds*, Roger Tory Peterson Houghton Mifflin, 1980

Songbirds in Your Garden, John K. Terres, Crowell

The Bird Feeder Book: An Easy Guide to Attracting, Identifying, and Understanding Your Feeder Birds, Donald and Lillian Stokes, Little, Brown and Company, 1987

The Bird Watcher's Diary, Edgar M. Reilly and Gorton Carruth, Harper & Row, 1987

The Bluebird Book, Donald and Lillian Stokes, Little, Brown, and Co., 1991

The Experts' Guide to Backyard Birdfeeding, Bill Adler, Jr. and Heidi Hughes, Crown Books, 1990

The New Bird Table Book, Tony Soper, David & Charles, Ltd., 1973

Wood Notes: A Companion and Guide for Birdwatchers, Richard H. Wood, Prentice Hall, Inc., 1984